Quickstyle

●

Quickstyle

HOW TO EXPAND, ENHANCE, AND UPDATE YOUR WARDROBE WITH ACCESSORIES

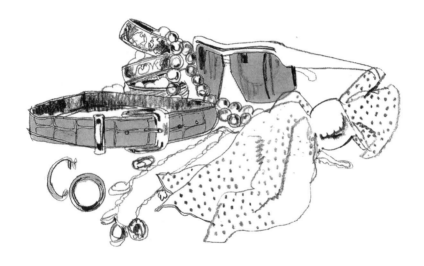

CHRISTINE KUNZELMAN

ILLUSTRATIONS BY
JACKIE DOYLE–BONETTO

VILLARD BOOKS • NEW YORK • 1995

LIBRARY OF CONGRESS CATALOGING-IN-PUBLICATION DATA
Kunzelman, Christine.
Quickstyle:
how to expand, enhance, and update your wardrobe with accessories
Christine Kunzelman.
p. cm.
ISBN 0-679-42941-7
1. Dress accessories. 2. Clothing and dress.
3. Fashion.
I. Title.
TT560.K85 1994
646´.34—dc20
94-11699

Manufactured in the United States of America on acid-free paper

9 8 7 6 5 4 3 2

Book Design by H B Production Services, Inc.

To my wonderful husband, Shelly Schwab,
for making all my dreams come true.

ACKNOWLEDGMENTS

THERE ARE many people who contribute to the writing of a book and their contributions come in many different forms. I appreciate this opportunity to recognize those who were there for me and made this book a reality. I begin with Evelyn Dallal because she is the one who got me on track with a single word—"accessories." Thanks to Phyllis Melhado for her sincere friendship, never-ending encouragement, and Rolodex of sources. To Regis Philbin, the "king" of daytime talk shows, who has made ten years of live television *always* exciting. To Kathie Lee Gifford for her wonderful kind heart. To Michael Gelman, who won't be satisfied until we've made over the world in one of his new and creative ways; to two of the most dedicated producers, Joanne Saltzman and Rosemary Kalikow, for so many fun segments; to Dennis Swanson for giving me my first big break on TV; and to Steve Friedman for making one of my TV dreams come true. To Amy Andrycich, my fantastic assistant. To my agent, Connie Clausen, for her knowledge and direction; to my editor, Diane Reverand, who from the first time I met with her believed in this book. To Bridget Byrne for her words and organization. To Jackie Doyle-Bonetto for the perfect illustrations. To Ken Kalunian for keeping his promise—which I am still holding him to. And last and most important, to my best friend and son, Erik Kunzelman. My wonderful new family, Kerry and Kyle Schwab. My supportive and loving second family, the Miguelezes. My inspirational sisters, Susan Everett and Pamela Everett, who are always there for me. To the memory of Jo Anne Armenio, who taught me the real meaning of being a friend; how I miss her. And to all the rest of my family and friends, for being the best fan club anyone could ever ask for.

I appreciate and love you all.

CONTENTS

Quickstyle

●

1

The Power and Pleasure of Accessories

I CAN CHANGE PEOPLE—not with plastic surgery, not with psychotherapy. I make people look good and feel good about themselves with my styling advice.

This advice is plain and simple—a straightforward message about how to learn to dress-to-impress by using accessories with flair and imagination, without spending much money.

I've always loved fashion. As a child growing up in Southern California, I would cut out and dress up paper dolls, putting on fashion shows for my friends and family. As a teenager I lived for the arrival of my favorite fashion magazine, *Seventeen.* I would stay up the whole night trying to make myself look like that month's cover girl, using my makeup and clothes to adapt my appearance to the very latest pretty style.

I still feel that joy and excitement. As an adult I've expanded my enthusiasm so that I am reaching out to others with fashion advice.

I see the potential in everyone. I haven't met the person I can't make look better, whatever her size and shape, however large or small her budget. I feel confident of that every time I undertake a makeover. I see the entire person from head to toe and, equally important, the style that is inside her. I believe everyone has untapped style. You just need to learn how to use it, how to take chances, how to be adventurous, how to open up, so that the best things you feel about yourself can be revealed in your outer style.

When I appear as a fashion authority and makeover expert on *Live With Regis and Kathie Lee* or other national TV talk shows, I get an enthusiastic and grateful response. I've seen women cry with delight, stand up straighter, and take on a whole new persona after I've made just a few fashion adjustments.

My way of using accessories transforms. It's not a slowly evolving transformation. It doesn't take long. Sometimes I only have an hour, at best usually just one afternoon, to work with these women. All I use is a little knowledge I've acquired with time and experience. It's worked for me personally, it works for the women who appear on the TV shows, and, as you will learn from this book, it can work for you.

Getting dressed in the morning used to be a nuisance for me. Now it's an adventure. Creating the look that is attractive and suitable to the day ahead of me is a well mapped out adventure, because now I know that with each brief trip to my organized closet I can pull out a belt here, a bracelet or scarf there, and swiftly mix and match these accessories so that I can walk out the door feeling comfortable and looking great.

It took me time to learn that developing a sense of personal style has very little to do with religiously following trends and having a bulging bank account. It's no secret that some of the wealthiest women wear some of the worst outfits, but we all think that if only we had lots of money to spend we could look great. Throughout this book, I am going to show you how you can learn to look terrific without chasing every new trend and spending lots of money.

Finding your own personal style and making it work for your lifestyle and budget aren't as difficult as you might think. Just as you can learn to be a good cook from using recipe books, or become fluent in another language by studying, so you can take similar steps to discovering and maintaining your own style.

Although I always had this great love for fashion, I had to work at becoming an authority. I began by reading every fashion magazine I could afford and then every book. I learned skin care and makeup skills, but soon realized I couldn't stop there. I was interested in the whole person. I studied fashion and design at the University of California at Los Angeles. On completion of the course I opened a full-service salon, Panache Appearance Studios in Los Angeles, to provide a makeover service, attracting politicians, authors, television personalities, executives, lawyers, and homemakers.

My first television appearance was on *Hour Magazine,* hosted by Gary Collins. I demonstrated his best colors—then a hot trend, and a very popular and easy-to-understand way of selecting the most flattering clothing hues and tones.

That appearance brought requests for my expertise from other Los Angeles–based talk shows. I worked with Regis Philbin when he hosted his morning talk show in California and I became a fashion reporter for KABC-TV and KABC Talk Radio. Soon I was working on national shows including *Sally Jessy Raphael, Oprah,* and *Live With Regis and Kathie Lee.*

I have done well as a fashion authority on television because I understand people's comfort zones. My makeovers are the most popular because I relate to the whole person, not just to her coloring or hairstyle. I take chances and can instill in people the confidence to take chances with me.

Too many fashion magazines and fashion books are geared to people who are already knowledgeable about fashion. Most people who live and work outside the fashion arena are often daunted by the idea of fashion, thinking that it's something beyond their reach—too expensive and only for those already blessed with good looks and great figures. All women want to look good in the way they present themselves to the world as women, but they don't know how to do this.

I believe it's possible for everyone to learn how to have style. Dressing well is not a birthright handed out only to beautiful models the minute they come squalling into the world. Even the style they project, both on the fashion runways and in their private lives, is a skill, something that's as easy and fun to learn as a foreign language.

Everyone can acquire style if she takes the risk and works at it.

ACCESSORIES ARE THE ESSENTIAL TOOLS OF STYLE

THE QUICKEST WAY to style is through the use of accessories. That's why I wrote this book. Accessories give flair, panache, and pizzazz to any basic wardrobe. Accessories have always been part of fashion, but they are particularly important for the nineties. Everyone, regardless of her budget, is trying to be more sensible about how she spends her money.

Accessories take an old outfit and update it. A belt draped a certain way, a scarf in the newest texture, a brooch pinned at a different angle can alter the whole line and look of an outfit. You might have wanted to discard that outfit, because the hemline wasn't the length the fashion designers had decreed for this season, or because it wasn't the color deemed "in" by the latest fashion magazine, but now you won't. Accessories turn a drab dress into something eye-catching. The plainest outfit can be quickly enlivened with the addition of a shiny belt, a piece of sparkling jewelry, or even a bolder shade of panty hose.

Accessories bring a designer look to affordable clothing. Whatever your income, a whole new suit, dress, or coat is sure to represent a big bite out of your fashion budget. The latest design in an accessory, however, will give you a taste of whether this year's styles are really for you, without your having to rush into that more expensive decision of purchasing a whole outfit.

Accessories are style—style you can create yourself. Accessories give you flexibility. They are the ultimate mix-and-match tools. Your choice of accessories and the way you wear them make a bolder statement about who you are and what you like than the basic clothing on which they are displayed.

This doesn't mean you should buy every gimmicky fad item in the hope that it will make you look up-to-date; nor should you buy something just because it looked good on a celebrity. Though celebrities can be a great source of inspiration in your quest to develop style, you must establish your own style, not a carbon copy of someone else's.

Beware the chipper saleswoman who talked you into those spangly earrings. Remember the last time you fell for that? Haven't those ear-rings just stayed in your drawer because they kept catching in the neck-line of your clothes, felt too heavy, or perhaps simply looked too tacky? It's not that you looked any different when you got home; it's just that away from the saleswoman's persuasiveness, you recognized the reality of your own style and knew that those earrings didn't suit it.

In this book I'm going to give you confidence in that sense of your-self. I'll show you how to reorganize your closet, so that getting dressed each day will be both less of a hassle and more of an adventure.

I'll help you select which of your accessories to keep and which to discard. By organizing your closet, thinking about what styles really ap-peal to you, and facing up to mistakes, you'll build the confidence to go with the style that is right for you.

I'll advise you about which accessories are essential. The essentials work day in, day out, giving you a sense of security about how you look. When mixed and matched, they provide a much wider choice of styles to work with.

I'll give you lots of money-saving tips about creating your own ac-cessories. I'll suggest different places like flea markets, gift-wrap depart-ments, and hardware stores where you can hunt for inexpensive items that make great accessories.

I'll describe how you can add whimsical touches by using acces-sories in imaginative ways. Remember, there are no firm fashion rules. Fashion is created by the imagination, by people's constant desire to ex-periment, change, alter, try something different. Accessories are the tools to help you take these steps to create your own fashion, your own style, in your own way.

I'll talk about the celebrities who dress well—and some who don't—so that you can learn how to use those celebrity images you admire to your own best advantage. I will show you why Candice Bergen is a good role model and Madonna isn't. I'll show how style isn't limited by age, explaining why Angela Lansbury's confident elegance makes her eye-catching even when she's in a room with such beautiful young stars as Michelle Pfeiffer or Winona Ryder.

I'll not only help you create, update, and perfect your own style by using accessories, but also teach you how to slim down or add height to your appearance.

I've put all my years of experience together to show you that expensive designers don't have to dictate your fashion look. Of course, they must be looked to for innovation and high style, but I will show you how to take the ideas they promote and adapt them to suit your lifestyle and to enliven and enhance your appearance, while allowing your own personality to find its true expression.

We women have worked long and hard to earn our rightful place. We no longer need to let designers tell us what to do. In fact, designers are recognizing this, learning to observe and listen to us when they shape their styles.

We are in control. So have confidence. Discover from this book how the style that is right for you is the style you like, the style with which you are comfortable, the style that is appropriate to your lifestyle and budget.

In the process you'll find style, your style, great style, "Quickstyle"!

2

Reshaping Your Wardrobe to Suit Your Lifestyle

HOW MANY TIMES has this happened to you? You know that you possess the perfect jewelry, panty hose, and shoes to enhance your most attractive outfit for that special affair. But when you go to your closet your accessories are a mess—panty hose are tangled, shoes are in a jumble, and you can't imagine looking either elegant or pretty.

Not only don't you have the right accessories to complement the outfit you're planning to wear, but your closet is stuffed with items that seem useless for any occasion. And it's been like that for years!

In exasperation, you crowd that pile of seemingly useless stuff back in the closet, and push and strain to shut the door on the chaos, telling yourself you'll deal with the problem later. Yet the very next time an important party, business meeting, or family celebration comes around, you find yourself faced with the same old jumble—and the next time, and the next!

What's your excuse to yourself? Probably you reassure yourself by imagining that the elegant-looking women you admire have not just an instinct for fashion, but also plenty of time to put their look together. That's not really the case. They've learned how to achieve personal style, how to keep it, and how to create it at a moment's notice as the occasion demands.

It's not as difficult to achieve this talent as you think. If you break down the approach women like these employ into simple, easy-to-tackle steps, you'll find that you, too, can almost effortlessly be stylish, even at short notice.

In my career, conducting countless makeovers with thousands of women from diverse backgrounds with all sorts of different lifestyle demands, I've proven to them that the acquisition and maintenance of style is easier than they think, as you'll find out if you follow my guidance.

ORGANIZE YOUR QUEST FOR STYLE

YOU'LL NEED to set aside a few hours, so choose a day when your significant other is going to the ball game, or an afternoon when the kids have gone to the latest hit movie. Make sure your dog has a good big chew-bone so he's not demanding to be walked, and perhaps a small handful of catnip for your cat will keep her from poking her nose in every corner of the closet you're about to empty out and reorganize.

You'll need to make a few small purchases ahead of your task. If you don't have any of the following items already on hand you'll need:

⊘ **A long, hanging see-through jewelry bag.**
You'll need at least one bag—maybe more, if you feel you have a lot of jewelry. These bags are divided into clear zippered sleeves and pockets. They roll up, and come in various sizes. The larger, two-

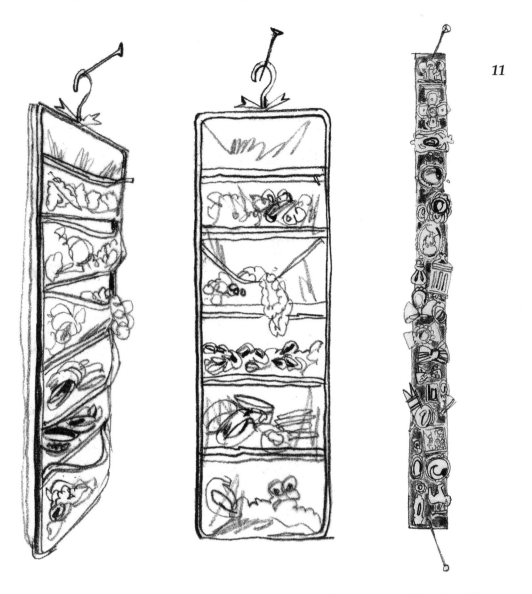

foot-wide, bags are the best for closets, but you might also like to add one or two of the smaller, six-inch-wide, bags, which are great for travel and can also be used for makeup. These bags are available in most notions, department, and closet-organizing stores.

⚙ **A piece of wide, heavy grosgrain ribbon.**
This should be about three inches wide and as tall as your closet, or at least as high as you can easily reach. Buy the ribbon, like the hanging jewelry bag, in a fabric or department store. You will be nailing this ribbon inside your closet as a place to display your pins and brooches.

✪ **A few sturdy three-inch nails and a hammer.**

✪ **A glue gun or Fabric Tac glue by Beacon.**
I've found that this permanent glue is really the best adhesive for use on wood, plastic, glass, and fabric. Most fabric, craft and hobby stores carry it.

✪ **Inexpensive metal stacking trays.**
However much shelf and drawer space your closets have, you will find these wire trays very useful for storage. They can be found in any hardware, do-it-yourself, or home-furnishing store.

✪ **Plastic storage cubes.**
These cubes are another inexpensive tool to help create more space and a great deal more order in your closet.

✪ **A belt hanger.**
Your closet may already have built-in hooks on which to hang belts, but if not, or if you prefer, buy a belt hanger while you are in the department or closet-organizing store. I think the straight ones (hanger-style), which have about eight hooks, are better than the round ones, which don't allow such easy access to the belt you may need.

✪ **A tablet of 8 1/2-by-11-inch lined paper.**

✪ **A pen.**

✪ **A clipboard.**

✪ **A piece of ribbon or string.**

✪ **A large mailing envelope,**
  at least eleven by fourteen inches

TURN A PAGE IN YOUR SEARCH FOR STYLE

Every time you see a fashion look you like in a magazine or catalogue, tear it out. (Well, don't do it in the doctor's office, unless you ask first, but you know what I mean.) Whether it's an advertisement or editorial copy using models, or a paparazzi shot of a celebrity, if there's an element of style you like or an image of how you'd like to look, save it. It doesn't matter whether the look is wild and outrageous or subdued and retiring. The only thing that matters is that something in the picture caught your eye. It doesn't matter what the model's age or ethnicity, or whether you think you could—or would really want to—wear the clothing. It just matters that you like the way it looks. Collect as many of these pictures as you can. I'll soon be explaining what to do with them.

USE CELEBRITIES AS YOUR GUIDE TO STYLE

In addition, think hard about the celebrities you're drawn to, because they're the first thing I'm going to have you focus on.

Name five celebrities whose style you admire. Jot down the names on your note pad. Who do you think looks well put together? Whose clothes do you wish you had? Think of their overall look. Think of how their choice of look reflects their personality. Think of how their appearance both fits in with and enhances their career and their lifestyle.

For example, are you a *Murphy Brown* fan? You like the show, not just for its up-to-date satire, but because every week its star, Candice Bergen, has such a pulled-together fashion profile.

As Murphy, Bergen looks very professional, as a successful career woman should, but her appearance also reflects the risk-taking quality in the highly competitive newswoman's personality. She achieves this look by adding just a little bit of an edge to a very classic foundation. It's a look that reflects the personality of both the character and the actress, someone whose confidence in her working skills allows her to speak her mind and who is comfortable enough with her beauty to wear her hair any way she chooses.

Bergen's clothes are simple and clean-cut, but they are always accessorized with wit and a touch of daring—her jewelry might be real or faux, or a mix, but it's always placed in the most eye-catching spot, just as her scarves are always wound in clever knots or coils, caught up casually by a great pin, or perhaps left to flow free if she's striding into the office in a particularly feisty mood. She wears mostly solid-color clothing, adding a contrastingly colored or printed silk scarf at the neck. Sometimes these are square scarves, folded in half with the point in front, which she then wraps around the neck of a jacket and ties, either in front or at back, creating a serious ascot look. Sometimes, inside a blouse collar, she will fold the square on the bias, rolled up tight and then tied around the neck. If she is wearing a top with a rounded neck, she will tuck the scarf in so that just one inch shows all around. This brings color and attention to her face by creating an appealing frame.

She is very imaginative about how she wears pins. She often likes to wear a bold pin at the neck of a buttoned-up blouse. The blouse collar is turned up and the pin is fastened over the top button, which holds the collar stiffly in place—another good face framer.

Her earrings are usually simple in form and solid in color and she matches them well to her varied hairstyles. When she wears her hair up for daytime, she'll sport a variety of interesting shapes, either plain or with a gemstone, but always controlled, confined, nothing dangling. When her hair is styled down and loose, she will wear longer drop earrings that move as she moves. In the evening she feels free to break those rules, but hair up or down, earrings long or short, her sense of proportion is always correct.

She is also very astute about how to use color well: a bright green gem brooch with a multicolored scarf will contrast well with a neutral-color suit; with a black suit she might choose a big, bold, bronze-beaded necklace, worn short and high to cast a tawny glow on her face.

Think about how her necklaces lie in easy contrast to her dress or suit neckline, or how her belt always seems to accentuate, rather than detract from, her elegant figure.

If you find her style appealing, put her name on your list.

Or perhaps you prefer the way actress Janine Turner dresses on the quirky television series *Northern Exposure.* Casual, outdoorsy, the look

CANDICE BERGEN

JANINE TURNER

we think of as an embodiment of an L. L. Bean catalogue, as though life were always a comfortable, happy, leisure-filled weekend. She looks relaxed and wholesome, fresh scrubbed, natural. It's not surprising that she was also picked to star opposite Sylvester Stallone in the as-big-as-the-all-outdoors thriller *Cliffhanger*, and that Ford has selected her as its spokesperson.

In *Northern Exposure*, which is set in Alaska, the accessories Turner wears denote warmth and practicality. Wool knit hats in solid collars are worn firmly pulled down so that only the smooth bangs of her hair show. People who wear everyday casual clothing can identify with her use of color to liven up sensible cold-weather gear. She knows that a berry red scarf will bring a warm blush to her cheeks, that a royal blue or hunter green turtleneck under a blouse will strike a bright, positive note, as will primary-color wool mittens. In her private life she obviously doesn't have to wear the layered look suited to the TV series, but she still maintains that wholesome, relaxed appearance with clean-line clothing, understated makeup, and traditional, small accessories.

Model Christie Brinkley, with her all-American, apple-pie looks, also falls into this fresh and natural category, though she's a bit more urban, and displays more of a groundbreaking edge (perhaps because she was married to the singer Billy Joel and moved in the music world, where hot and cool trends wax and wane very fast).

Don't you just love the way she always manages to wear ultra-chic sunglasses and to tilt hats at a rakish angle? Her look works because, though her clothes are very up-to-the-minute, she's not overpowered by the styles she chooses, and she has that knack of using accessories to make a snappy comment, not to detract from the main statement.

She likes to wear hats of all shapes and styles—a cowboy Stetson with a traditional bandana scarf tied around the brim or around her neck; a big-brimmed straw hat in summer; a small beret pulled down low, with her hair tamed to lie smooth and a piece of black ribbon tied simply around her neck; a baseball cap with her ponytail pulled through the opening at the back. When she wears a hat, that's where she wants the attention to be, so any other accessories, such as earrings, will be kept small and simple.

A very different look that might appeal to you is that of miniseries queen Jane Seymour. Not only does she usually play romantic roles, but she dresses romantically in real life, a style that Amy Irving also favors.

When you think of both these actresses you think of soft, flowing, perhaps flowery clothes, and details and accessories to match that mood—a lace pocket square, a pearl choker, a cameo pin on a velvet neck ribbon, a flower pin on a lapel—all touches of old-fashioned femininity that give these women a romantic aura. No boxy, mannishly structured business suits for these pretty women.

In contrast, superstar Madonna is often clearly pushing to be ahead of the trends. She's always attracted to the new and the avant-garde. She constantly reinvents herself with her use of style and accessories. She's been all over the place. When she first became famous there was still a touch of sweetness to a look that she had clearly picked up from English teenagers. She wore lots of layers of exposed petticoats, slips, and camisoles, and then she layered on the jewelry, particularly chains and crosses. This was the era of one of her better films, *Desperately Seeking Susan.* She then began to strive for traditional glamour, aping the style of

CHRISTIE BRINKLEY

 MADONNA

Marilyn Monroe with marcelled hair, sleek, tight clothing, and glittering jewelry—she wore rhinestone necklaces and earrings and even tried to revive the feather boa. Remember her Academy Awards show appearance in this mode? Later she returned to a different take on the teenage schoolgirl, perhaps influenced by her role as the female ballplayer in *A League of Their Own*. She wore knee socks with culottes, and bows and pigtails. She always keeps moving, pushing each look further and further until it becomes a vulgar parody of the original concept, at which time she breaks away into another completely different style or, if she's lost for ideas for a moment, tests out just how much nudity the public will tolerate.

It's not necessary to be as bold as Madonna, but a touch of shock value here and there can be exciting and attractive—a Maltese cross on a long cord, silver- and metal-studded belts, distressed leather vests, the newest shape in sunglasses whether it's day or night, rainy or sunny.

The music industry has a very strong influence on fashion. The Grammys are a much more eye-catching evening of innovative fashion than the Oscars. There's usually a certain flung-together, tousled appearance to glamorous singers, which, far from being unappealing, merely reflects their love of a hectic lifestyle. This look may seem too extreme for the average person, but the Grammys are a great arena in which to observe how the trends born on the streets can be glamorized to the maximum. Later that glamour will be filtered down and readapted to everyday fashion, perhaps showing up in your closet. The Grammys started the trend for tennis shoes as an acceptable, if somewhat different, footwear with tuxedos. This is the event from which one huge, shoulder-dusting earring evolved into an everyday accessory. When first worn by music stars at the Grammys, that earring was probably too big, too outrageous for most of us. But we liked the idea nevertheless and so we've adapted it in a smaller, more discreet way. Most of us wouldn't wear a whole military or band uniform as many pop stars used to do, but many of us now find a touch of that military look woven into our wardrobes— a webbed belt, a twist of gold braid, a medal worn as a pin. So music superstars such as Natalie Cole, Janet Jackson, Whitney Houston, and Gloria Estefan and country singer Wynonna can be a definite source of inspiration.

If that's how you see yourself, hold that image in your mind, or better yet, find and save photos of those energetic celebrities.

By contrast you might be attracted to the calmer, more tranquil mode, which is never dull when it is personified by someone like the late star Audrey Hepburn. Even as a gamine ingenue she knew the strength of classic sleekness, yet as she matured she always displayed the unique touch that prevented her neat white gloves or tidy pillbox hat from seeming staid, and she always picked up on the best of each era. Few people have looked so elegant in jeans worn with either a plain white fitted T-shirt or a big classic man's-style shirt. Her *Breakfast at Tiffany's* look will

AUDREY HEPBURN

always be striking—a basic black, sleeveless sheath dress worn with medium-length pearls, long black gloves, and a big-brimmed black hat and black-on-black sunglasses, with her wrists wrapped in rhinestones. The long cigarette holder wouldn't impress today as it did back in 1961, but everything else would still resonate as classic elegance.

Personally, I'm influenced by the confident, classic look I see worn by TV correspondent Diane Sawyer and by the eternally eye-catching Jackie Onassis.

Diane Sawyer took the staid executive look that female anchors had inherited from their male colleagues and made it chic. She softened it. She sometimes opted for turtleneck sweaters in place of jackets, and at other times chose an open-necked, strong-pastel blouse with a thick matte gold chain inside the collar—a less fussy alternative to the bow-necked blouse. She doesn't wear a lot of jewelry, but she uses color well as an accessory. She's conducted an interview in as simple an outfit as a tailored gray shirt with black slacks, providing the color with a turquoise sweater tied casually around her shoulders—the perfect accessory for the occasion. She doesn't wear long earrings. Hers are small and traditional, but always look very expensive. She does use scarves, but always controlled, tucked into a neckline, never free-flowing, and they are usually in solid colors or in traditional Hermes or soft Armani prints.

Jackie Onassis always wore extremely tailored, extremely expensive clothing. Her slacks and sweaters were simple and elegant. She didn't favor bright colors, but she loved good fabrics—cashmere and silk, textures that gave extra impact even to basic black, navy, and neutral-color clothing. She popularized oversized sunglasses in the 1960s and she stuck with that look throughout her life. She was always seen wearing hats and gloves, not caring if they've moved in and out of popularity on the fashion scale.

I also like Diane Keaton's retro look, which uses old and new classics rearranged to her own satisfaction. She likes to juxtapose contrasts. She wears an old-fashioned print granny dress with canvas tennis shoes or heavy combat boots and pearls. She'll accessorize a very contemporary business suit with an extra-wide belt over the jacket, carry an antique purse, and wear granny glasses. She has the talent to create a personalized look that is unexpected and always a charming, creative surprise. Even if some fashion authorities criticize her for being a touch silly, she is always refreshing. It's clearly her own choice, a confident self-expression. I admire that.

So there are fashion role models to be found all over, in television, film, music, and politics. You see them every time you turn on the set, go to the movies, or pick up a magazine.

ASSESS YOUR CHOICE OF CELEBRITY STYLE

THINK ABOUT which celebrities appeal to you, then write down your top five choices. Looking at that list, you'll probably notice they have some things in common. Record what shared traits you see.

Perhaps it's a fondness for the same color themes—muted hues or bright jewel shades. Perhaps it's print fabrics or simple one-tone clothes.

Perhaps your chosen stars are adorned with many accessories or they are just wearing a few simple pieces. Analyzing these stylish role models will help you to understand the basics for your own personal style.

Start thinking about what your style has been up until now and take stock of the outfits that have worked well for you and those that haven't.

TAKE A LOOK AT THE STYLE IN YOUR WARDROBE

LIST THE FIVE OUTFITS you've worn most the past year:

As you get ready for work, which suit do you reach for when you want to make the best impression? Which dress do you always get compliments on at business meetings? What outfit do you put on when you don't feel great and want to look slimmer and prettier?

When you get home in the evening what do you change into—a long, loose skirt, a caftan robe, your favorite sweats, or a big, roomy shirt and leggings?

On the weekends, when you are running errands, catching a movie, or going out for a casual lunch, is it your blue jeans, denim shirt, and blue blazer that are your favorite combination? Or is it the big turtleneck wool sweater over slim pants? Or maybe a long skirt worn with a T-shirt top and a vest? Or are you usually in a leotard or tights and big sweatshirt?

When you go out on a date or to a party, do you choose a tuxedo-style black suit, a soft, flowing silk shirtwaist dress, or a knit tunic and pants?

For any formal daytime ceremonies such as weddings, special anniversary luncheons, and civic duties, do you choose your Diane Fries–style ruffled print dress, your Nolan Miller *Dynasty*–style brocade suit, your St. John–style knit two-piece, or your Armani-inspired unconstructed pantsuit?

When you go out to dinner, do you nearly always reach for the same black pantsuit? You like it because it's comfortable, it's classy, it works. Or maybe you've had lots of wear out of a zippy scarlet skirt that you pair with a shapely black jacket. You get compliments when you're seen in both of these outfits, so write them down on your plus list.

List the five outfits that have hung untouched or barely worn in your closet for the past year. They're the easiest ones to find because they always have dust on the shoulders!

Remember the three-piece suit with the traditional bow at the neck that looked dated from the day you bought it? One for the minus list.

The flowered long T-shirt and matching leggings that looked romantic in the catalogue, but make you feel both overweight and overdecorated, like an overstuffed chintz chair, when you wear them at home? Another outfit to go.

The leather motorcycle jacket that all the fashion magazines suggested as a must-have to pair with blue jeans and white T-shirt, but which proved too stiff, too confining, and too much of a gimmick and made you realize you should have bought a traditional soft-leather bomber jacket instead? If you don't wear it, you don't need it.

The slinky black dress you bought when you started your diet because it was going to look just right when you took off ten pounds? But you didn't, so it doesn't. It's too tight, certainly not good for dining out in. That's an ongoing dust-gatherer.

Your dyed-to-match pink satin suit and shoes? The dyed-to-match era has long gone. Move that combination out.

There are no compliments for that harsh purple jumpsuit with the pleats that never quite lie flat, since it never gets out the door of your bedroom. Every time you try it on, you rip it right off again and throw it back in the closet. Another for the minus list.

Making a right-and-wrong list like this will help you define your style. It may be hard to admit that there are mistakes in your wardrobe, but once you do, everything becomes a lot easier. We all have a few fashion skeletons in our closet or chest of drawers; so admit to them and put them on this list so you can give them away or sell them at the next swap meet. Facing up to mistakes will help you admit that succumbing to extreme fads or buying on impulse is usually not for you.

Now that you've pared down to the wardrobe basics, you can take a look at your accessories, which are going to highlight your choices.

Make a list of your accessories, subdividing them into the following categories:

Everyday Accessories

Would you feel naked, even if you were just going to the post office, if you weren't wearing your watch and a thin gold necklace? Or maybe you know you are ready to face the world every day when there are small pearl studs in your ears, a lizard belt threaded around your waist, and black-on-black sunglasses shading your eyes. If you're confused about which of your accessories fit this category, look at the little pile of jewelry you take off each night, the belt you hang on the most accessible spot, the shoes that are in the front of the closet—the things that you wear almost every time you dress. These are your everyday accessories.

Evening Accessories

Once the sun goes down, is your grandmother's beaded 1920s purse always in your clutch? Put it on this list. And add those rhinestone drop earrings and the clunky pearl bracelet that catch the gleam of candlelight when you're on that special date. Maybe you have rhinestone buckles that can be clipped to your evening shoes, or a faux-gem, soft gold, or milky pearl chain that can be worn as a necklace or a belt. Perhaps you like to adorn all your fingers with rings when you don't have office duties or home chores to deal with.

Sentimental Choices

These are the accessories you are really fond of and that you wear when the mood strikes. Maybe once a week you like to wear a locket with your loved one's picture in it. Maybe you have some lovely Navajo turquoise earrings that were given to you by special friends. Of course, you'd wear them when you met the friends for lunch, or perhaps even if you knew you'd be talking to them on the phone. And then you might have bought yourself a pair of brushed-silver triangle earrings, as much as possible like the ones you admired on Katie Couric when you watched her host the *Today* show one morning. It gives you a lift to wear them on days when you want to feel especially lively and bright.

Accessories Rarely or Never Worn

You swore you'd look glamorous in those green cat's-eye sunglasses, but somehow they made you look like somebody's dotty aunt, so they never saw sunlight. That clunky ankle bracelet seemed enticingly exotic and rather daring in the store, but whenever you put it on, the "slave" look seems not just politically incorrect but absurd.

Now that you've sorted out the items in your closet and chest of drawers you want to keep from those you don't, it's time to take stock of yourself again.

UNDERSTAND THE FASHION STYLES YOU LIKE

NOW take out all those torn-out pages you've been collecting from the magazines, those pictures in which something caught your eye. Spread them out on the floor in front of you and recognize what they have in common. When pictures of stars you like are arranged beside fashion editorial pages and advertisements, you will notice that there are similarities in your choices.

Did you choose mainly pictures of waifish, crop-headed brunettes in body-hugging flowered slips with dangling daisy earrings?

Or did you pick svelte, tidy blondes in gem-bright colors and gleaming jewelry?

Or staring back up at you are there statuesque beauties, their posture softened by the neutral tone of their firmly structured jackets and the drape of their pearl-and-gold chains?

Are the accessories small, medium, or large? Are they simple and basic, or are they ethnic and colorful? Do they jump out at you from the picture, or do you have to look hard before you notice them? How many accessories is each model wearing? Which are similar to accessories you already own? Which ones would you like to own?

Write down the common elements. You may have collected pictures that denote one clearly defined style—the romantic look perhaps—or you may have chosen looks that can be grouped into three or four entirely different styles. Don't see a single look as a symbol of narrow thinking or a varied choice as confusing; recognize your selections as a way to begin to identify your likes and dislikes, a step into the open, an expression of the style that has been hidden within you.

EVALUATE YOUR LIFESTYLE

NOW DESCRIBE your lifestyle. Make a chart for yourself by drawing a circle and dividing it into slices like pie wedges to represent, in percentages, how your life is divided.

How much time do you spend in casual clothes, such as the relaxed pantsuit you might wear to a movie?

How much of your day do you spend in business clothes? Probably, if you think about it, considerably more than the standard "nine to five," because your work clothes are put on long before you get to the office, and business meetings often run into the evening without the time to change. (Though, as you'll learn later in this book, clever use of accessories can make for a completely different evening look, without your having to get out of the dress or suit you've worn all day.)

How much time do you spend in really dressy clothes? Do you at-

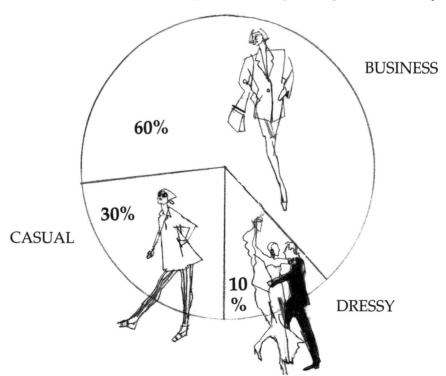

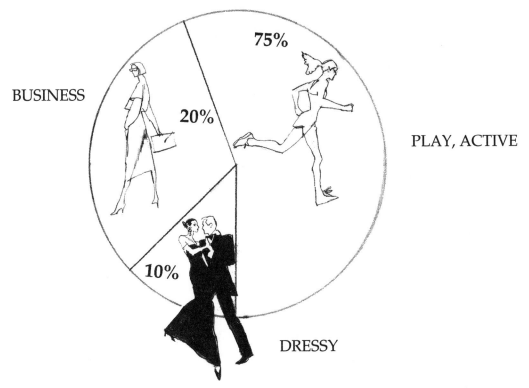

tend many functions where your escort is looking really dashing in black tie?

How much time do you spend in active wear or play clothes? These are the clothes you wear around the house or to the gym.

You must fill the whole pie to total 100 percent of your day. (What you wear in bed is your own business.) So perhaps you might figure it out a bit like this:

You're an office administrator: 60 percent of your time is spent in business clothes, 30 percent in play clothes, 10 percent in dressy clothes.

You're an aerobics instructor: 75 percent of the time you'll be in active wear, while the remaining 25 percent you will divide between your business and party needs.

You may be surprised when you see how your chart looks—perhaps you can use colored pens for each section to reflect the different feeling you want to express in each area of your life. You won't be alone if you realize your clothes and lifestyle are completely out of balance. During my career I've met working women who don't have any dressy outfits, even though their work often takes them to evening meetings where a more festive appearance would be quite appropriate, and I've also met women who stay home much of the time, yet hardly own any active or play clothes, while their wardrobes bulge with cocktail wear.

I used to have the same problems. Fashion-wise, I was as confused as everyone else. One month I'd see a look I liked and try it, only to change the next minute when I saw someone else traipsing around in another outfit I found appealing.

I called my style "roving." It was all over the place! If *Vogue* told me to wear three belts for the current season, you can bet I'd be first in the store to purchase that trio. I was always searching for the newest, the latest, the greatest. And I felt urged on in this manner because people were always asking me, "What's new? What's hot?" I felt I had to be wearing the new and the hot to be on top of every trend. When I watch some of my old tapes from TV appearances, I have to laugh at all the different phases I went through.

I was just as susceptible as you may be to the assurance from a convincing saleswoman that a pair of huge drop earrings looked wonderful on me. I would get caught up in the moment and imagine how great these rivers of glitter would look on my next evening date, but then the minute I returned home with my purchases I'd be disappointed. They didn't seem to go with anything I had and they didn't even look that good anymore on their own. I could probably have found something among the jewelry I already owned that would mix and match with my outfit and look just as clever and up-to-the-moment.

It wasn't until I'd been in the fashion business for a long time that I figured out how to be objective. If I got tempted (and of course I still do sometimes) I'd hold up those big swinging earrings while I was still in the store and ask myself, "Would Jackie O., Diane Sawyer, or Diane Keaton wear these?" If I heard, "No," then I'd put them back. But sometimes I'd hear, "Yes," and it would be clear that however newfangled the look, this was something I could and would wear.

Now I realize that what's best is what works for you. That doesn't mean you can't love the way something looks on somebody else. I love dangling earrings—on other people!

I've often seen them worn with business suits, and they looked great. Think of Jane Fonda. She has a wonderful collection of long earrings and she doesn't just wear them for evening. You'll see her at the baseball game, rooting for her husband's, Ted Turner's, Atlanta Braves, wearing long earrings with sporty clothes. She looks so good I sometimes try on similar earrings, but each time, I realize they don't work for me. They're not within my comfort zone.

CONSIDER YOUR OVERALL STYLE

SO NOW your list is growing, each choice and consideration helping you to learn about yourself, what you like and don't like, what you should keep in your wardrobe or discard.

You're getting closer to realizing your own personal style.

Now that you're beginning to get that sense of self, it's time to make all those accessories that were cluttering your closet and scattered in your drawers or hidden in your jewelry box fit your style.

When you checked over and listed every accessory to see if it was an everyday piece, an evening piece, a sentimental favorite, or a mistake, you probably divided them into appropriate piles—pins here, sunglasses there, necklaces there, earrings somewhere else.

Make sure you've done this with all items—scarves and hats, pocket squares, stockings, shoes, handbags, belts, gloves.

Subdivide—break down the piles into smaller piles.

Scarves can be divided by color—solids in one group, prints in another. Then they can be divided again by shape—oblong from square, long from short.

You've already divided jewelry into day and evening wear, so you can either put those sentimental favorites into the appropriate category or keep them in a separate group.

Stockings can be divided by color, then into sheer or opaque. And make sure that you keep and subdivide both socks and knee-highs into their own piles. Think how annoying it can be to grab what you think is exactly the right color and texture panty hose only to find on unraveling that they are merely knee-highs and can't be worn with the dress you've decided on.

MAKE A STYLISH WISH LIST

TAKE THAT PAD of lined paper and the large envelope you bought and fasten them to the clipboard. Attach the ribbon or string to the pen and tie that to the clipboard. Hang this clipboard in your closet. You could slip it over a hanger or hang it on a nail in your closet wall.

Now take another look at those pictures you collected of the looks you like. If it was the pearl necklace the model was wearing that caught your fancy, then write that down on your pad of paper.

This is the start of your shopping wish list. Of course, you may not get everything you want—real pearls and real diamonds, for instance—but if that's what you want, write it down; it's something to work toward!

When you've written down all your wishes, don't throw those pictures away. Slip them into the large envelope for future visual reference. Then add to the list accessories you feel will work with the outfits you like.

Maybe you've always loved a gray-and-cream-checked skirt, but you rarely wear it because you realize each time you put it on that it would look better with gray nylons, and you still haven't bought them. So write "gray nylons" on the list.

Before you go to the mall you can check this shopping wish list and the magazine pictures and you will see both what you need and what you like.

This list serves the same purpose as a grocery list—it stops you from wasting money on useless things you don't really want. Wasteful closet clutterers and drawer crowders will be gone! Your money will go to accessories you'll love and wear often and long—perhaps even forever. This will save you time and money.

The most expensive accessory is the one you never wear. A twelve-dollar pair of earrings bought on sale but never put on are ultimately more expensive than a fifty-dollar pair that are so perfect you wear them three times a week. If you wear them long enough, you can figure out that eventually they cost nothing, but are totally valuable! Jewels beyond price are what we all wish for!

This list will stop you from making shopping mistakes and help you make shopping investments. But don't feel that this more ordered approach, and the recognition that you can and do make mistakes, locks you in. It's a tool that is your friend, not your enemy. This method will help you feel confident and in control, open to new ideas, and more prepared to try looks you see on those you admire. You'll feel secure enough to sample a variety of the styles that appeal to you, borrowing from Madonna and Amy Irving and Jackie Onassis and Diana Ross. You will probably find that your comfort zone is more varied than you imagined. The freedom to mix and match is one of today's blessings.

REORGANIZE YOUR CLOSET IN STYLE

NOW THAT you've thought through everything and stacked all your accessories in piles, it's time to put everything back in your closet, but not in the same old way.

Jewelry

Don't toss your jewelry back into that bulky old jewelry box. If you have one, give it away to an aunt or a niece, or, if you are really fond of it, display it on top of the piano. Those old-fashioned boxes just don't work—they take up too much space, they hardly hold anything, and you can never see clearly or find quickly what they do hold.

Your jewelry is moving to a new home, into those long, hanging, see-through jewelry bags you bought. I've found that this is the most efficient way to keep jewelry neat and accessible. Break down the jewelry to fit into the bag's different compartments. If you have some very tiny, easy-to-lose items like stud earrings, you might borrow a few Ziploc bags from your kitchen, pop in those small items, and then put the bag in the appropriate compartment. Gold earrings go in one sleeve, silver in another, evening in another, and so on.

Then sort your bracelets and necklaces. This way, when you want something gold you can go straight to the "gold earring" or the "gold bracelet" sleeve, and there it is.

If you own a lot of long necklaces, and don't want them to tangle, it may be better to hang them up on extra-large nails that you can hammer into any dead-wall space in the closet. One heavy nail can hold about six necklaces and those big nails can also work as a place to hang your hats.

While you have your hammer out, nail that piece of wide grosgrain ribbon inside your closet door or at the closet supports, so that it is visible. Now gather up your pins, fabric flowers, and jacket clips, because this is where you are going to display them, so that you won't have to grope around blindly for that suitable accessory. It will be in clear view.

You can have fun deciding how to display these pins—perhaps by size and shape, perhaps by texture, or maybe just in an attractive pattern, mixing and matching the jewels, the pearls, and the flowers.

Scarves

If you don't have enough shelves or built-in drawers in your closet, the wire trays and plastic boxes you bought will do the trick as the place to put your scarves.

Keep the scarves in the piles you have already created—prints divided from solids and further divisions by size and shape. In addition, you can stack your pocket squares and any pieces of ribbon you have. Although you may not have any ribbons, you probably will soon, because later in this book I'm going to show how ribbons you can buy at your local fabric store can be used in many imaginative ways as wonderful accessories.

Panty Hose and Stockings

Trays and boxes are also perfect storage areas for stockings and panty hose, which I feel are best kept rolled up and tucked into a ball. It's handy to use unopened packets of stockings as dividers to keep the various styles and textures apart. Stack up your stockings with the sheers in one place and the opaques in another. Stack by color within these categories, keeping the navy, the black, and the deeper shades of gray away from each other, because it's often difficult, when the light isn't perfect or you're in a rush, to tell these colors apart.

I'm sure all of us have peered hard at a pair of tights, questioning which of these shades they are, made our choice, then gone outside to work or a meeting and found we were wrong. The midnight blue pair you thought you'd selected were in fact plain black.

I remember when I was working on ABC's *Home* show and had to be dressed and out of the house by four A.M. when it was still pitch-black outside. One day I wore a navy suit with olive nylons! I wasn't planning to make any offbeat fashion statement; I just didn't see what I'd done until I was under the bright lights of the television studio. Luckily, the wardrobe staff helped me correct my mistake by providing me with some more appropriate stockings. Now that my closet is better organized I'm not so likely to make such an error, though I always carry an extra pair in case of mishaps.

Labels can be an additional help here. Put the navy nylons in their own Ziploc bag and label it "navy," and do the same with the black and the gray. I even Ziploc and label my evening stockings with a clear "P.M." to distinguish them from the ones I wear during the day. You won't have to stick your hand in them to see how sheer they are, perhaps risking a run. It's a time-saver too.

Belts

Hang belts according to day or evening wear and subdivided by color and width, either on hooks in your closet or on the belt hanger you purchased.

Purses

Shelves are, of course, an appropriate place to store purses, but if you don't have enough space, then inexpensive plastic storage cubes work perfectly.

Again, make those day-versus-evening and color distinctions. As you'll learn when I discuss purses later in this book, you could probably do without many of those you own, and instead just invest in a few all-purpose ones.

Shoes

If your closet doesn't have built-in shoe racks, or you don't have space for shoe racks on the floor, you can use plastic cubes to store your shoes. Remember, the idea behind rearranging your closet is to make it easy to see and to get to everything you have. If you do put your shoes in plastic boxes, label them clearly. The best way is with bold marker pens. Use different colors. I suggest black for day, red for evening, and green for weekend. Write in large print what the shoe is. For example: "black loafer" or "brown pump, two-inch heel," and so on.

Gloves

Use drawer space if you have it or place your gloves in plastic storage cubes. Try not to store your gloves in the pocket of your overcoat or warm jacket because if you do you'll only end up wearing the same pair whenever you wear that one particular garment. Besides keeping you warm, gloves are an attractive accessory in themselves that can brighten a variety of outfits. A winter-white suit worn with black gloves and black

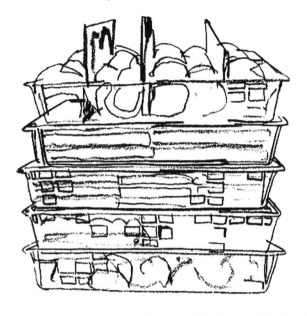

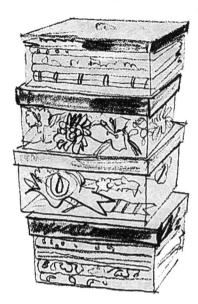

pumps is very elegant. If those black gloves were hidden away in the pocket of your black coat, you might never think to try them this other way. Divide gloves into day and evening use and then, if necessary, make other subdivisions.

Did you have enough space for all this? If not, think about where else in the house you can neatly store clothes. Often there is a hall closet or even an underused kitchen cupboard. Better to utilize that than over-stuff your bedroom closet and risk creating that jumble you've just worked so conscientiously to eliminate.

Now stand back and take pride in the job you've done.

You've moved a long way to learning more about your own fashion style and you've organized in such a way that you won't feel frustrated and confused by the jumble when you're rushing to get ready for work, or while your kids are complaining about what's in their school lunch boxes, or when you're trying to look great for your arriving date while your cat doesn't seem to want to eat his dinner because you haven't mixed in his vitamins carefully enough.

You'll be able to take that extra moment to tend to those needs, be-cause you'll know exactly where to find the scarf that picks up the subtle check in your suit, or the necklace that is exactly the correct length for your evening dress.

3

Essential Accessories for Enduring Style

WHAT ARE THE ESSENTIALS?

AN ESSENTIAL is any item that's simple, classic, and ever-usable.

Don't get misled into thinking that the essentials are boring. Just as every good kitchen must be stocked with flour, sugar, and salt and every efficient office with a phone, a computer, and pencils and pens, so every wardrobe must have essentials in it to function well.

Essentials are the items that are always safe to be seen in, always appropriate to wear, always available as a solid foundation on which to build your own style.

Once you possess these essentials you can indulge in any trend, try any gimmick, go for something new and extra each year, because the essentials will be there for you every day, year after year.

If that seems dull to you, think, for example of how a brilliant architect, whatever his ultimate creation, has to start with plain bricks and mortar. A good foundation is behind every grand edifice. The same applies to fashion.

Since you want essentials to last, it is important always to buy the best quality you can afford. Eighteen- or fourteen-karat gold will last forever. Fourteen-karat gold plate will wear away. Good-quality leather will age gracefully and take on a whole new character and patina as it is polished over the years. Plastic or imitation leather will crack, split, and peel.

KATHIE LEE GIFFORD has such an unharnessed personality you might think she would favor flashy accessories, but in fact she is very faithful to the essentials. She likes classic, high-heeled pumps, pearls, conservative earrings. She also has a sweet, sentimental favorite, a gold Tiffany heart that she often wears on a medium-length chain. She also knows how to be resourceful. I remember one morning when she felt that short, double-strand pearls would look better with her outfit than one long string. She simply doubled over the necklace, used a safety pin as a clasp (which would be hidden by her long, thick hair), and achieved the look she was after. "If only Barbara Bush could see me now!" she quipped before going to the set.

Game show personality VANNA WHITE, whose way with clothes became an integral part of *Wheel of Fortune,* is someone we think of as exuberant and a little flashy. But actually she is very conservative in the way she uses accessories, sticking to the essentials and never going for anything faddish or far-out. In fact, in some ways she is stuck in an early eighties time warp and might benefit from risking being a little more nineties.

I can't stress strongly enough the importance of owning the best-quality essential accessories you can afford. Doing so will save you hours of confusion and doubt. They will prove pleasing in themselves and will enhance everything else you wear.

Most of us accept that our wardrobe should contain essential clothing—a black dress, a white T-shirt, and a pair of black or tan slacks—but when we turn to accessories we throw out that concept, imagining that they should make a bolder, less conventional statement.

We think that if we pile on jazzy hats, clunky belts, or overpriced ornate shoes we can instantly create a high-fashion look. The same rules that apply to dresses and suits also apply to accessories. You need essential accessories—simple stud earrings, a gold chain, a plain leather belt, a string of pearls—to make your outfits work for days, evenings, and weekends.

Much as you might resist the idea of these accessories' plainness and simplicity, you'll soon see that they really are the most wonderful items in your wardrobe. They are ageless—they'll work for you whether you are fifteen, thirty-five, or seventy-five.

They'll work for any budget—it's possible to find, as I have, a one-dollar string of fake pearls at a street stall in New York that looks almost exactly the same as a department store item selling for over forty dollars.

They are ultrafunctional. You'll wear these accessories until they wear out.

Following are my suggestions for essential accessories.

ESSENTIAL EARRINGS

The essential earring is as necessary as your watch. It's as much a finishing touch as your lipstick. It's not about making a statement; it's about completing a look. These are the earrings you need to wear to job interviews, important business meetings, corporate dinners. They are always appropriate. While fashion moves all over the place, there are some standards you need to adhere to when you don't want to worry about making a mistake. These essential earrings are never a mistake. Your long wooden-bead earrings may be your current favorites, your up-to-the-moment fashion statement, but there are many occasions in life when you must rely on the tried and true. No accessory wardrobe is complete without some of these essential items. Select several from the list below, making sure one choice is a simple nondangling stud. Whatever your

choice, make sure they don't catch on anything. You should be able to wear them comfortably at all times, whether in bed, at work, or playing sports. They will go with everything, from bathing suits to party dresses. If you have pierced ears, all these styles come in posts; otherwise they work just as well as clip-ons or screw-ons.

Take into account your size.

If you are petite—five feet four inches or under—or small-boned, select small earrings.

If you are of medium height and weight, choose medium size.

If you are big boned with a fuller frame, opt for large. Keep in mind that because these are essentials, they should never be too large—nothing that dangles below the chin. Remember, it's not hair length that dictates the size you select, it's your build and proportion.

Essential Daytime Earrings:

❂ *Gold.* Any small clip-on, post, or button earring in shiny, brushed, antique, or hammered gold.

❂ *Pearl.* A single pearl, a double, a small cluster, or a tiny drop in white, pink, yellow, or beige tones.

❂ *Silver or Bronze.* A geometric shape—square, triangle, octagon, or rectangle in shiny, brushed, or hammered metal.

❂ *Hoops.* Any gold, silver, pewter, or bronze pair; plain, without trim.

Essential Evening Earrings:

❂ *Flashy rhinestones.* These are essential because they can make almost any outfit look very dressy. I have a pair of rhinestone hoop earrings that I've had for years. Whenever I feel that my evening outfit needs a boost, I put them on. Instantly I feel glamorous, ready to have a good time.

❂ *Huge pearls.* Don't think of pearls as just being white. Pearls come in many shades—cream, ivory, pink, and yellow tones, even black. Pick whichever shade you feel best suits your skin tone. Use your lipstick shade as a guide—oranges, corals, and peaches suggest you'll look best in the yellow and cream shades. If your preferred lip color is mauve, plum, or rose, then choose the pink and clear-white tones. Black pearls can be an essential earring for anyone, but this is one place where you need to invest in the real thing to avoid the unsightly peeling of the fakes.

❂ *Large hoops of gold or silver.* You may think that hoops are a style that goes in and out of fashion, but I consider a pair of hoop earrings an essential accessory. From dainty wedding-band hoops to large bold ones, you can build a whole look around hoops.

I have a vivid memory of ALI MACGRAW on a television show. I can't remember what outfit she was wearing, but I do recall how huge gold hoops set off her short geometric haircut, making her stand out from everyone else on the show.

❂ *Dangling faux gems.* If you are not comfortable with the flashiness of rhinestones, these bright faux gems, which gleam and glisten under evening lighting, are an elegant alternative. Whether ruby, emerald, sapphire, or a mix of jewel tones, they add instant glamour in the same manner as rhinestones.

In the evening, all your essential earrings can be longer, bigger, brighter. The size and the sparkle depend on your personality. When the sun goes down you can afford to turn the mood up. At least one pair of evening earrings will make all the difference to your wardrobe. Just how bold you will want to be depends on your own comfort level.

ESSENTIAL NECKLACES

These work for both day and evening wear. They can be worn individually, grouped together with other essential necklaces, or, as you will learn later, heavily layered or adapted in numerous ways to express your own creativity.

✪ **A single short strand of pearls.**

✪ **A sturdy gold or silver chain,** either choker length or resting just above your collarbone.

✪ **A medium-length**—about eighteen to twenty-four inches—gold or silver chain.

✪ **A long**—thirty-two inches—strand of pearls.

✪ **A long string of black cording,** the same length as your long pearls.

Forget that song about diamonds being a girl's best friend. Pearls are much more user-friendly. Real or fake, long or short, small or large, worn alone or mixed in, pearls are a must-have.

A pearl choker can brighten up the most conservative of suits, as BARBARA BUSH proved. It can be worn day and night, as Britain's QUEEN MOTHER knows. She's still eye-catching though she's over ninety, and she's never without her favorite triple strand of pearls. And BARBRA STREISAND also knows that pearls work almost anywhere. She's successfully worn a multi-strand choker with everything from T-shirt and jeans to a flapper-style evening dress at the Academy Awards show.

The long pearl necklace is particularly versatile, for day or evening. It can be worn loose, wrapped in a choker, or tied in a knot at bust level.

You can also sling it sideways across a jacket, use it as a belt, adorn it with ribbons, bows, lace, or pins, or mix it with other chains.

When you select a chain, the choice of gold or silver is up to you, and

everyone can wear both; but if you can't decide which is best for you, here's my rule of thumb:

If you have a yellow skin tone with warm-brown, golden-yellow, or copper-red hair, wear gold. If you blush easily at racy movies, then your skin tone's pink and you'll look better in silver. Silver also complements dark neutral-brown, black, silver, gray, or white hair.

Buy chains that are sturdy enough to be adorned with charms, so that you can try some of the more whimsical ideas I'll be telling you about in a later chapter.

You'll find that the length of black cording can also be dressed up with charms and pins. It's only twenty-nine cents a yard and it can make quite an impact, whether worn alone or mixed in with other necklaces.

ESSENTIAL RIBBONS

- ✪ **Ivory.**

- ✪ **White.**

- ✪ **Black.**

This is another inexpensive fabric-store purchase I'll be giving you more ideas for later on. Buy a yard each in velvet, satin, and grosgrain and you'll find many uses for them—as chokers, hair ornaments, even belts.

ESSENTIAL BELTS

○ **Brown,** medium-width, in natural-color, smooth or skin-textured leather.

○ **Taupe or bone,** medium-width, in smooth or textured leather.

○ **Black,** medium-width, in smooth or textured leather.

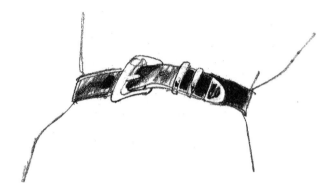

All these belts should have the following qualities: They should be classic, not ultrashiny or adorned with any glitz or gadgetry. All the buckles should be small, either gold or silver, or leather covered. The belts don't have to match your purses or shoes, because their simplicity allows them to blend in easily with the rest of an outfit. The most versatile belt will probably be the brown one, which can be worn with almost everything from blue jeans to summer dresses. The medium width of the belts is important because they will slip easily through belt loops.

A leather belt will always improve an outfit, looking much smarter than the matching belt that comes with a dress or slacks. Remember always to buy the best quality you feel you can afford because a good-quality belt makes an outfit look instantly more expensive. Ralph Lauren's belts are some of the most beautiful classics. His designer belts in reptile skin sell for upward of five hundred dollars, while his casual belts range in price from fifty to one hundred dollars. If these prices are beyond your budget, you can still aim for a similar look, by checking out his belts for style first and then shopping for good replicas.

ESSENTIAL PINS

Every wardrobe needs at least two essential pins: one that works for day as well as evening and one that's primarily for evening wear; one in pearl, the other in rhinestone. That's my advice.

I love pins and I think people should invest in a whole wardrobe of them. Pins are very much an individual choice, reflecting your personality, and can be collected over the years. But for your essential accessories, start with these classics.

❂ **Pearl.** You will find that a simple pearl pin, medium size, in whatever shape appeals to you, will work both day and night. You can wear it on a jacket lapel to work or on an evening gown at a party. You can attach it numerous places—to a ribbon choker, at the neck of a blouse, on the pocket of a shirt or the cuff of a sleeve.

JOAN LUNDEN likes to wear pearl jewelry with her structured blazers and suits. I admit I sometimes find her ultraperfect tidiness a little disconcerting if I'm tuning in to *Good Morning America,* still blurry eyed and in my pajamas. But these pearls do bring a softening touch to her excessive neatness, as do the pins she wears on her blazer lapels. Still, I'm always wishing she would do just one thing that is more individualistic or different. Just once, maybe two contrasting-toned ropes of pearls or two or three pins on her jacket lapel!

❂ **Rhinestone.** Rhinestones denote glamour. Their sparkle, under evening lights or candlelight, reflects a shimmer and radiance onto your face that convey the fun and special feeling of being dressed up and enjoying yourself.

Size and shape depend on your own preference.

A rhinestone pin on your lapel can turn a navy or black business suit into a cocktail outfit. It can also add an instant dressy touch if you place it at the center of a turtleneck or high on the top button of a blouse with the collar standing slightly up. Or you can pin it to the shoulder of a basic dress, or over a belt buckle to create shimmer at your waist.

Don't overdo rhinestones. Two rhinestone accessories are the most you should ever try—perhaps earrings and a bracelet, earrings and a belt buckle, or shoe buckles and a pin.

ESSENTIAL POCKET SQUARES

These pocket squares will suit your daytime outfits:

❂ **A man's white hanky** in cotton or linen.

❂ **A black pocket square** in any soft fabric.

❂ **A lace pocket square** preferably in a neutral color.

You can often find good used hankies or armchair doilies, which will wash and bleach up like new, secondhand at swap meets. Two capfuls of ammonia in your wash will eliminate yellowing and restore brightness. You're not going to cry into these hankies, but you will find you usually want to wear one.

White squares look great with a blue blazer worn over a white T-shirt and jeans.

Black squares go well tucked into the pocket of a tweed, herringbone, or checked jacket.

Lace can soften the menswear look of any business suit.

There are many ways to wear these squares:

• You can put all the points stuffed down into the pocket for a serious, professional look.
• You can fold them into a traditional square, with the squared-off edge peeking out of the pocket, for a corporate look.
• You can pull the center of the pocket square down, inside the pocket, leaving the points out, for a soft relaxed look.

• The more of the pocket square that shows, the more casual the look.

• You can even use a thin oblong scarf as a pocket square, with a long train hanging out, to create a very high-fashion look.

The essential pocket square for evening wear is gold or silver. This is a very inexpensive way of livening up a black or white blazer and picking up the mood of glittery earrings.

As I will tell you in more detail later, these pocket squares aren't limited to your jacket breast pocket. They can be worn in the low front pockets of a longer jacket, blouse, or cardigan sweater. They can tuck into the pockets of your blue jeans. They can be worn in vest pockets.

ESSENTIAL SCARVES

Next to earrings, the scarf is probably the most popular accessory of all time. Most people own several. It's an ageless, versatile accessory that never goes out of style. Ways of wearing scarves may change, but the scarf itself is always adaptable. I often find that people own numerous scarves, but lack the ones that rate as essentials. Ideally, they should be cotton, gauze, chiffon, silk, fine wool, or cashmere, but it's also possible to find very attractive scarves in today's softer synthetic fabrics that fold and tie very naturally.

These are the ones I feel you need:

- A thirty- to thirty-six-inch square in a neutral solid color—black, camel, navy, cream.
- A thirty- to thirty-six-inch print square—dots, stripes, flowers, or whatever else suits your taste.
- A thirty-six-inch or longer oblong solid or print scarf in one of the neutrals.
- A fifty-four-inch or larger square scarf to use as a shawl or wrap.

Big, square scarves are ultraversatile. They wrap into ascots, tie into chokers, sling into ties, knot into sailor squares.

These scarves can be worn over blouses, under blouses, and even instead of blouses under high-necked, buttoned-up jackets. They can be draped over sweaters, though I suggest avoiding that draped-over-one-shoulder style, which looks contrived and always has to be fussed with.

You can get some good ideas from looking at celebrities who wear scarves well.

I admire how *Today* show host KATIE COURIC uses large square scarves in prints and solids and a variety of colors to soften the professional business look of her clothes. She wears print scarves with solid-color suits or bright colors with severe navy or gray pinstripe suits. She uses a scarf like a mock turtleneck, tucking it into the top of a jacket, blouse, or sweater with just two to three inches of the scarf showing. Because most of the time the television image frames her from the shoulders up, the scarf enhances her face much like a colorful mat around a picture.

CANDICE BERGEN also uses scarves very imaginatively on *Murphy Brown.* She knows how a well-placed scarf can draw attention away from or cover up a neckline that isn't as young as it used to be.

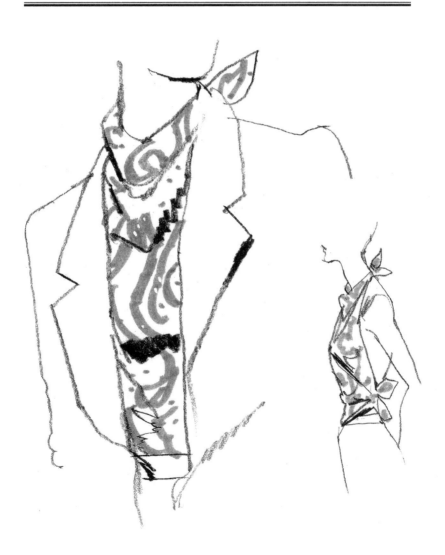

A print scarf, whether worn around the neck or threaded through belt loops and used as a belt, can really brighten up a solid-color outfit.

Oblong scarves are just as versatile as squares and often wind and twist better into Windsor knots or bows, fold more naturally under blouses, and flow more dramatically when you move.

If you buy a big enough square, or make one yourself from a piece of heavier woolen fabric, you will find that this accessory often serves you as well as an expensive evening coat. (Nothing looks worse than a woman pairing a dressy evening gown with a casual daytime coat). If you own the essential fifty-four-inch-or-larger square, in a solid black, dark brown, or gray scarf, shawl, or cape, in a warm fabric, this can become your evening wrap.

ESSENTIAL GLOVES

❂ **Black leather or brown leather** with a lining. This is the best choice for daytime. Buy a pair, preferably not too short, so that two or three inches of the glove will go inside your coat sleeve. It's best to buy ones that are lined; lined leather gloves are both more comfortable and more practical. Choose a cashmere lining if you can afford it.

❂ **Knitted, in a basic neutral color.** Always buy the best quality you can. These knitted gloves will work with your more casual clothes and weekend wear.

When you try on gloves, work the fingers around to make sure they fit well and are not too stiff, so you will be able to use your hands easily.

❂ **Black satin or rayon.** These are for evening wear. Select two different lengths of black satin or rayon. One pair should be long enough to go over your elbows to wear with a sleeveless, off-the-shoulder, or strapless dress. These gloves give your evening dress an air of sophistication. Think of Audrey Hepburn.

The other pair of evening gloves should just reach your wrist bone. Make sure they fit well and have an attractive fastener, such as a pearl button. These gloves look great with both daytime and evening suits, accessorized for evening.

I think evening gloves are very important. They show off jewelry well, particularly items like cuff bracelets. Gloves ornamented with decorative buttons or small pins are elegant and sexy.

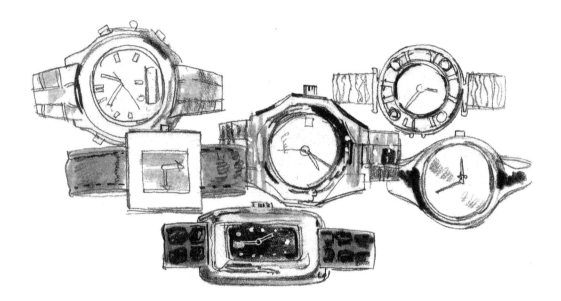

ESSENTIAL WATCHES

Many people notice your watch before they notice anything else you are wearing. In our culture watches have become status symbols. Like the cars we choose to drive, they reveal our sense of self-worth. Though the choices are varied and you are by no means limited to owning just one, for the essential list I recommend this:

✪ **A classic "timeless" watch with a standard face,** a black, oxblood, or brown leather strap, or a gold or silver band. Rolex or Cartier watches are the ultimate, but since most people can't afford the real thing, you will find that many brands make good, inexpensive replicas of these classics. Men's styles are often more traditional and are therefore a good buy. Your essential watch can be worn with every outfit in your closet and at every time of day. If you love watches you can then buy additional styles to wear in various ways, often mixing one or two together as you might with other jewelry items.

ESSENTIAL STOCKINGS AND PANTY HOSE

Stockings are not only a necessity, but they are also the underpinning of your whole look. We've gone way past the days when nude nylons were the essentials. Nowadays nude nylons, whether stockings or panty hose, should be a minority item in your closet. Even the essentials require a much wider variety of colors and textures. Stockings tie your whole outfit together, set off the rest of your accessories, and make a statement in themselves.

Stockings are also a much less expensive way of giving variety to your feet than a whole wardrobe of different shoes. For instance, instead of investing in black-and-white spectator shoes, it is clever, more affordable, and equally attractive to wear opaque white nylons with your black pants and your black heels or flats.

Opaque black stockings are definitely a woman's best friend. This look makes everyone appear taller and slimmer, and works much better with skirts and dresses than sheer stockings. Whether at work or at play, we all tend to be more active these days and, and if your skirts are short, sheer, or revealingly slit, you will feel more comfortable and attractive if your legs are not excessively exposed. Opaque stockings are not just more flattering, but are also easier to care for. You can toss them into a pillowcase or laundry bag and wash them in a cold and gentle wash cycle. Don't tumble-dry them—you'll never get rid of the lint and the heat will break down the fibers, causing runs. Just hang them up to air dry. Most opaque stockings for winter are a heavier mixture of nylon and spandex, but if you need coverage even in the warmer seasons cotton opaques are available in light neutral or pastel colors.

CNN's fashion guru ELSA KLENSCH is another on-air personality who knows how to dress appropriately for her age, and she always wears dark-color nylons that pull her outfits together. She favors the classic and the conservative in her dress and accessories and is not tempted to move out of this comfort zone even though she daily confronts the extremes of international fashion. I watched her interview KARL LAGERFELD, the flamboyant designer. He was, as usual, wearing his silver hair in a ponytail and very dark-tinted, black wraparound glasses. She was in a simple navy dress with oval red earrings and, of course, dark navy nylons. She's discovered how to be regal.

Sheer stockings, of course, can have great impact if you have great legs.

I've spent a lot of time in green rooms, the holding areas in TV studios for the programs' guests. The more popular or striking the guest, the more crowded the space. I was there once when RAQUEL WELCH showed up, and suddenly everyone who worked in the building needed to come into the green room to get a cup of coffee. She was showing off great legs to best advantage in a very short skirt, ultrasheer nylons, and very high heels. Everyone was in awe. But of course, most of us don't look like Raquel and need a little more coverage from our nylons.

For most women, medium-sheer hose are probably the best for hiding the shaving scars, moles, and broken veins we'd rather not advertise. Check the back of the panty hose package for "stretch fiber" content: the heavier the fiber content, the less sheer they will be, the longer they will last, the more imperfections they will cover, and the less they will bag. For example, 10 percent Lycra holds up much better than 2 percent. It will also be a thicker nylon with better coverage. Remember, it is best to stick to the classic colors—bone, taupe, black, and navy.

Buy the best-quality nylons you can afford. They last longer and look better on your legs. If you get at least ten wearings out of a five-dollar pair of stockings, that's much better value than a very cheap pair that bag around the knees, feel unpleasant to the touch, and often run almost the moment you put them on—or even before. Before you wear your panty hose I suggest taking them out of the package, wetting them, and then placing them in the freezer overnight. Let them thaw and you'll probably find that they last longer.

Your essential stocking wardrobe should contain all of the following:

❁ **Black, opaque.**

❁ **Black, sheer.**

❁ **Nude or flesh-colored**—just a shade darker than your own skin—medium-sheer.

❁ **Taupe, medium-sheer.**

❁ **Navy, opaque.**

❁ **Navy, medium-sheer.**

❁ **Gray, opaque.**

❁ **Gray, medium-sheer.**

❁ **Bone, medium-sheer.**

❁ **White, or cream opaque.**

ESSENTIAL DAYTIME SHOES

✪ **Black pumps.**

✪ **Black flats.**

✪ **Luggage-colored brown pumps.** This is that wonderful golden-brown color found in luggage or natural hides. It is not too dark or too light so that it works all year long, not just when you wear browns, but with any and every other color in your wardrobe. This is also a nice alternative to bone shoes when wearing white or pastels.

✪ **Luggage-colored brown flats.**

✪ **Taupe or bone pumps.** (Taupe is the color between gray and camel. If you're not quite sure of the color, look in the hosiery department for direction because it's one of the most popular colors for panty hose.)

✪ **Taupe or bone flats.**

Women probably indulge a weakness for shoes more than any other accessory. This is fine if you have an unlimited budget—though take note that buying thousands and thousands of shoes in every color and style didn't bring Imelda Marcos ultimate happiness!

You only need a few essential pairs, so if you are on a tight budget, don't put the emphasis on your feet. Lime green shoes might work for a prom, a wedding, or on Zsa Zsa Gabor, but neutral tones look better in practically all other instances.

Just as with your essential belts, buy flats and heels in black, brown, and taupe. Follow the same rules by buying the best-quality leather you can afford and take good care of your shoes. Good-quality leather shoes can be reheeled and resoled to give you longer use. Keep them well pol-

ished and the heels free of scuffs. You can use brown or black markers to hide scuffs and then polish over. The easy-application, roll-on-bottle polishes are timesaving, but not as good for better leather as the old-fashioned cake polishes and a little elbow grease.

Although it may sound boring, both your flats and your heels should be plain and unadorned, with the toe and heel enclosed. They will work all day long and into the evening with skirts and pants, both casual and dressy. I assure you that if you stick to the essentials you will always have the right shoes. Avoid white shoes; taupe or luggage color always looks richer.

England's PRINCESS DIANA and Monaco's PRINCESS CAROLINE both have duties that demand they spend a lot of time on their feet. Like most Europeans they understand the value of good-quality simple shoes and handbags—the essentials at their best. The European way of accessorizing is to buy the best you can afford, even if that means only one purchase for the entire season—though, obviously, that doesn't apply to these princesses. ISABELLA ROSSELLINI has similar taste in purses and footwear. Everything she selects is essentially classic.

ESSENTIAL EVENING SHOES

❂ **Black leather or black satin pumps.** Dressy satin shoes are wonderful for evening. Buy very plain ones with a closed toe and no more than a two-inch heel. You can pick the shape of toe and heel you like, but keep the shoe plain. For sparkle you can add buckles, pins, or even earrings. If your budget won't allow this extra pair of evening shoes, your daytime black pumps will work just as well and can also be adorned with pins and buckles.

ESSENTIAL SUMMER AND WEEKEND SHOES

○ **Neutral plain sandals.**

○ **Plain, white deck- or boating-style canvas tennis shoes.**

○ **A pair of sports tennis shoes or cross training sneakers.**

Make sure the sandals you buy stay on your feet well enough so that you can run in them as well as walk. You can pair them with lightweight pants and shorts as well as summer skirts. A natural leather or luggage color is usually the best; it will look much richer with a casual linen or print summer dress than anything white.

Your plain white deck-style canvas sneakers also look good with long cotton skirts or dresses, and of course are perfect with pants, jeans, shorts, and sweats. They machine wash easily, but will last much longer if you let them dry naturally rather than use the dryer.

For more intensive walking and working out you need a more structured athletic shoe. There are shoes designed for virtually every purpose at most sporting-goods stores.

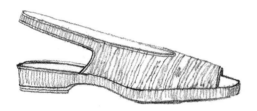

ESSENTIAL PURSES

✪ **A plain, medium-sized zippered purse in black or luggage-colored brown leather.**

This is the best choice for daytime. Most of us look like the hunchback of Notre Dame toting around a huge bag that tilts our shoulder and makes us walk lopsided. We suffer from "the big bag syndrome"! I used to be like that, too, feeling weighed down and awkward carrying a huge purse stuffed with all sorts of things I thought were necessary, but weren't. Because most of us are not six-foot-tall glamorous models, these huge bags overwhelm us and throw our appearance as well as our backs out of proportion.

Now I have scaled down to one medium-sized purse for everyday use. Get one too. You'll find if you redefine the essential contents (one lipstick will get you through the whole day!) you will be much more comfortable with this choice. Mine is black because I wear a lot of black, but if you lean toward brown, then choose a natural luggage-colored

leather. The bag should be easy for you to open and close, but a zipper is an essential deterrent to pickpockets. A bag with a double-stitched shoulder strap, one half inch or wider, that slings across your chest is the best investment, because it gets the bag out of your way much of the time, relieves stress on your shoulder, and deters potential purse snatchers.

Again, follow the rules about buying the best quality you can afford and keep your bag in good condition. Leather is always preferable to plastic. Look for riveted buckles and small studs at the bottom of the bag. The pocket inside the bag should be as deep as the bag, so it doesn't create a bulge when you put your keys and other items in it. These details will ensure that the bag is sturdy and will last longer.

One really good bag will serve you much better than a whole assortment of inexpensive ones, and you'll find it a great time-saver not to have to keep moving the contents of your bag from day to day.

❂ A small black envelope or a tiny black shoulder bag.

These are the best types of bag for evening use. Your choice can be leather, silk, or satin. It should be plain. For our essentials it is not necessary to bother with fancy rhinestones; plain black works best. You need only a few necessary items for evening—a lipstick, comb, compact, some

tissues. You don't need your whole wallet—though always carry some cash in case of an emergency; even the most fervently anticipated date can turn out differently than you imagined, and you may want to get away on your own!

✪ A large tote and a fanny pack or runner's pack.

This is the way to go for weekends. Though you can do without a huge bag for everyday use, it is handy on the weekend and, of course, there are women who carry one daily in addition to a purse because it can hold bulky items like those good pumps you don't want to wear on the long commute to work.

For winter weekends buy a tote bag in plain black or brown, in leather or a synthetic fabric.

For summer weekends buy a tote in a knockabout fabric such as mesh, straw, canvas, or clear plastic, because this bag is going to have to survive the great outdoors. In summer you can often find special offers from the cosmetics companies for attractive totes when you buy a certain quantity of makeup, so look for these in your local department store.

When Chanel and Prada design fanny packs costing up to seven hundred dollars you know that they are accessories that have caught on, mainly because they fit a need for the active woman of the nineties.

These little sacks that clip around your waist are great for travel and exercise because they leave your hands free and put no strain on your shoulder. Besides being perfect for long walking trips, hikes, and sight-seeing, a fanny pack is the best purse to take with you when you go grocery shopping or are out with young kids whose hands you need to hold.

Sports fanny packs come in high-tech fabrics and bright neon colors, but I recommend basic black. At an economical price, a fanny pack in either black leather or black nylon looks more sophisticated and goes with more outfits in your wardrobe.

Once you have acquired these essential accessories you will quickly appreciate how much easier it is for you to look good every day.

But your need for self-expression obviously demands that you go beyond the essentials to build an accessories wardrobe that is uniquely

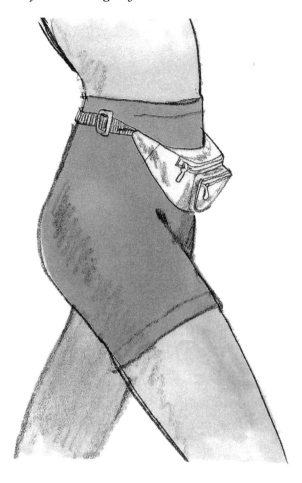

your own. In the next several chapters we will explore your many accessory options, help you select those that appeal to you, and suggest how to mix and match them with your essentials and your basic outfits to reveal your own personal style.

4

Jewelry Options to Reflect Your Individuality

PINS

I LOVE to wear whimsical pins even when I know I must appear serious and businesslike. For instance, when I was interviewing literary agents to represent me for this book I knew it was important to show my personality. Though I was wearing a business suit, I added a bright sunflower pin to the lapel. This whimsical touch drew the right agent for me. When she raved about the sunny pin, I knew she would understand the importance of accessories and this book's message, and we'd work together well. To confirm our arrangement, instead of a letter I sent her a duplicate of my sunflower pin!

Pins are a wonderful accessory because you can wear them in so many different places and mix and match them so creatively. I love small pins clustered together on hats, collars, pockets, or lapels. When you put several together, follow the rule that they must have something in common, whether size, color, or style.

WHY DON'T YOU TRY THIS WITH PINS?

Besides the traditional places to wear them—your jacket lapel and the neck of your blouse—try placing them in other spots:

✪ **On a low pocket.** A cluster of pins looks very striking on the low pocket of a jacket or cardigan sweater.

⊙ **On a turtleneck.** Place your pin slightly to one side on the collar or just underneath it on the shoulder or put a cluster of small pins together.

⊙ **On sleeve cuffs.** Small clusters of pins look striking and attractive here. And this unique placement will set you apart from the average lapel pin wearers.

⊙ **On the shoulders of blouses.** Small pins scattered around one large pin can create an attractive constellation effect. Many women pin on a butterfly or bee so that it looks as if it has just landed on a shoulder. I opt for being more original, with a flower or star pin, for example.

☼ **On a tie.** Group a number of tiny pins down the front of a solid-color tie, mixing them in with men's tie tacks. Or cluster them in the center or off to one side.

☼ **On the pocket of slacks or jeans.** This unexpected placement will always get you compliments.

☼ **Just below a belt.** Place the pin slightly off to one side of the buckle. It will look almost like part of the belt.

☼ **Attached to a bobby pin** as a hair ornament.

Be creative. Try:

☼ **A pearl pin,** clipped to the side of a long string of pearls.

☼ **Gold and silver pins mixed together.** If you do this it is always

best to follow through and also wear gold and silver earrings or bracelets.

✪ **Flower Pins.** Pin one or more flowers to your hat, your hair band, to a ribbon to wear as a choker, to a clutch purse over a clasp, into your hair, or use flower pins to hold up one side of the hem of a long romantic dress or skirt so that a lace slip or pretty stockings will be shown off.

Wrap a colorful scarf around your waist and pin a large flower to the front—you've just created your own unique belt.

If you want to give an antique touch to your flowers, follow a tip I learned from retro hat designer Louise Green. She buys fabric flowers in white and cream and then steeps them in a cup of ordinary tea. Brew a strong cup, dip in the entire flower or just the tip of the petals, depending on the look you want. Louise mixes her sepia-toned flowers with old pieces of lace and eyelet ribbons to trim her hats or make corsages.

ABC's BARBARA WALTERS is an excellent role model who has learned how to use accessories to help her stay looking much younger than she is. She knows how a scarf tied high at the neck or the special placement of a pin can draw the eye so that the inevitable flaws that come with age are disguised or minimized. On *20/20* she has successfully used a gold, pearl, and gemstone pin twice in the same night. The first time, she was at the anchor desk wearing a high-buttoned olive jacket with a pale pink scarf tucked into the neckline. The stunning pin was on the side of the jacket and was complemented by round gold-and-pearl earrings. During the show, in the taped segment where she interviewed BARBRA STREISAND, she had chosen the same style jacket in chocolate brown over a matching turtleneck sweater. The pin was in the same spot, right above her left breast, and she wore plain, round gumdrop-shaped pearl earrings. She understands that a dash of bright color in a scarf and a pin is better than a whole brightly colored outfit, but she never accessorizes to grab attention away from the person she is interviewing.

At the Emmy Awards show I saw one woman wearing a whole smattering of sparkling rhinestone pins on the shoulders of the black turtleneck she had paired with sleek black tuxedo slacks. She had created a very glamorous evening look. But be careful, because it's easy to overdo it. I noticed LATOYA JACKSON wearing a swarm of rhinestone lizard pins down the right shoulder of a black sweater and the right side of her black slacks. She looked overrun by reptiles!

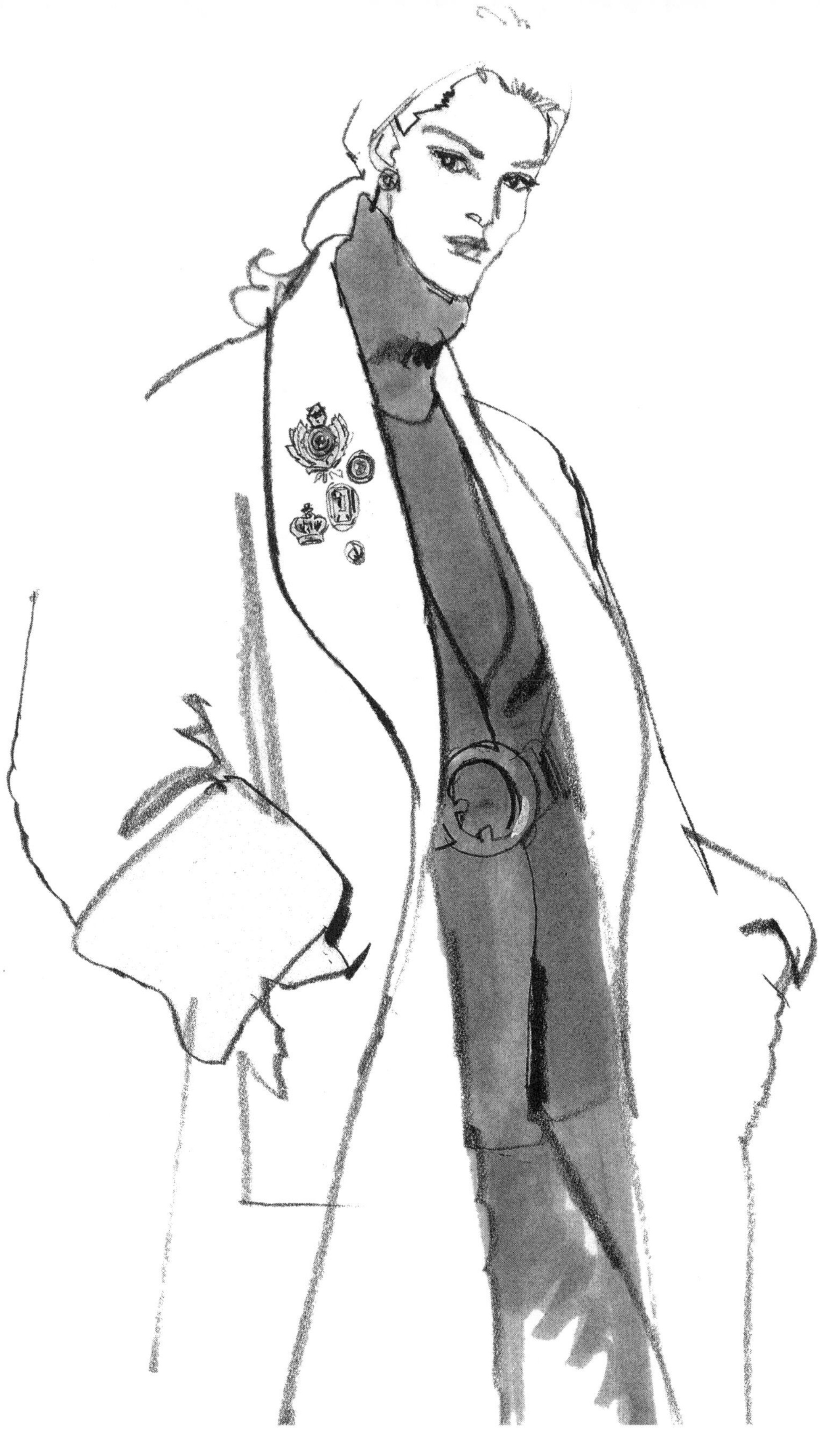

When Cristina Ferrare was the hostess of a popular Los Angeles morning talk show she often wore large colorful flower pins on her jacket lapels. These pins were so lively and bold that they began to irk the station's conservative general manager. He wanted Cristina to stop wearing them, but Cristina, being Cristina, went to her friends, the viewers, and asked them what they thought of her flower pins. They wrote and called in to say they loved them. So the flower pins continued to bloom on Cristina's lapels, much to the general manager's chagrin! Nowadays, when I run into her at Hollywood industry events, I always find she's wearing an interesting and beautiful pin on her outfit. It's an accessory touch I watch out for and admire.

✪ **Dough pins.** These don't just express your taste but show off your own artwork and cooking skills as well. They are simple to make. In fact, children love both making and wearing them.

Here's the recipe:

> 2 cups flour
> 1/2 cup salt
> 1/2 cup hot water

- Mix the ingredients and keep kneading until the mixture is really smooth and holds together.
- Roll out and cut into shapes with cookie cutters or to your own designs.

You can add any ornaments you wish—for example, twigs for whiskers or antlers on cat or reindeer pins, cake decorations or tiny buttons for eyes, and so on—just as you might if working with clay.

- If you are going to hang your design as a tree ornament during the holidays make sure to put a hole in it for the hook or ribbon loop. It can do double duty this way.
- After decorating, bake on a cookie sheet in a preheated 225-degree oven for three or four hours, until really hard.

• Once cooled, paint, if desired, with acrylics or nondiluted watercolors.

• Spray with shellac on both sides to preserve the dough. Several coats will give a very high gloss.

• Glue the pin to a pin back, available at craft shops and notions departments.

❀ **Antique pins.** Every era has had its own fashions in costume jewelry. Much of this older costume jewelry was well made and so there is a wide variety of pins to be found in antique stores and at swap meets, frequently in excellent condition and usually costing very little.

An old piece like a stickpin or bar pin is eye-catching when worn with a very modern outfit. Try thirties enamel and faux jewels or fifties plastic pins with your jeans or business suit.

❀ **Personal message pins.** Signal your tastes by using pins that reflect your interests. If you are an animal lover or a sports fanatic use your jacket lapel to display your fondness for dogs, cats, or horses, or golf or tennis.

You'll find these message pins always start conversations at parties.

EARRINGS AND NECKLACES

Almost all the same materials, whether stones, metals, or fabric, are used to create both necklaces and earrings. One accessory can be worn without the other, but as both essentially play off the structure and skin color of your face, you will often find that you've chosen necklaces and earrings that complement one another. But don't make the mistake of buying matched sets. When worn together, earrings and necklaces need to have some element in common, whether color, shape, or material, but they must also have their own clear originality; mixing your own favorites together is the way to create style.

ANGELA LANSBURY is a longtime Hollywood star with consistently good style. I imagine you have noticed, as I have, how she really stands out from the crowd when she appears at special Hollywood parties and on the Emmys or Oscars award shows. Not only are the evening dresses she chooses perfectly fitted to her tall, strong figure, but her jewelry is always carefully chosen both to complement the gown's neckline and her own short hairstyle and to make her look glamorous and youthful. I sat next to her at the Golden Globe awards show and noticed she matched her gemstones to her dress color—ruby earrings with a vibrant ruby dress. It could have looked predictable, but on her it was perfect because of the simplicity of both the jewelry and the dress. She doesn't always stick with the traditional. Hosting the Emmy show in 1993, she was wearing a very trendy monastery-look dress, but she didn't wear the expected big cross with it, just soft pearls. She had taken an up-to-the-minute trend and made it work for someone her age.

ELIZABETH TAYLOR, one of the last of the great stars who remains highly visible, sometimes still dresses like an old-time movie queen. One of the mistakes she makes is with her jewelry. Individually, much of what she wears is beautiful (if a bit too huge) but she tends to overdo it. When the stones are that big you don't need to wear so much. She also falls into that old-fashioned habit of matching the color of her jewelry to her clothes. When both are very ornate by themselves, put together they are overwhelming in their decoration. I sat close to her at dinner some time before her most recent marriage. She had just launched her Passion perfume line and was clearly dressed to promote it, in a purple beaded gown with diamond and amethyst jewelry. Because they were on Liz, the necklace, earrings, and bracelets must have been real, but worn as a matched set they looked like inexpensive imitations.

WHY DON'T YOU TRY THIS WITH EARRINGS AND NECKLACES?

⚙ **Mismatched earrings.** Earrings can even be successfully mismatched. This idea works as long as the two earrings have something in common, whether style, shape, or color. For instance, one hoop can be plain and conservative while the other can be smaller but decorated with a heart, pearl, or tiny key.

Be prepared to explain your choice if you do this. I love the look, but recently someone in the audience at a TV show I was appearing on thought I had lost the charms off one of my earrings. I had to explain the trend. Then she wanted to try it herself.

⚙ **Personal messages and designs.** As with pins, earrings are another accessory you can use to deliver a subtle personal message. It's much more attractive to signal your taste this way than by wearing an overdecorated T-shirt or one stamped with a message.

If you love the beach, wear shells. If you like the rodeo, sport tiny horses or miniature cowboy boots.

Add beads, rhinestones, painted wood, or miniature metal charms to plain hoops, clips, or screw-on chains to make your own unique earrings.

✪ **Ethnic earrings.** Every culture has its own style of earring—Native American beads and feathers, Russian and oriental gold fretwork and cloisonné, South Seas shells and dried seeds, Middle Eastern filigree and hammered metal. You can find these beautifully crafted accessories at street bazaars and gift and museum shops on your travels or in specialty stores at home.

I prefer the look of ethnic jewelry paired with casual summer cottons and linens, or with blue jeans and khaki and olive weekend wear. Some of the more elaborate dangles make an interesting combination when worn with evening dresses.

Always think about the neckline of your outfit when you choose earrings. Shoulder-dusting earrings are dramatic with a scooped V or open neckline, but they don't work with a cluttered, collared, or trimmed neckline. If your collar is fussy, wear simple studs.

Try not to wear very heavy earrings, particularly if you have pierced ears. The earlobes droop, people think you must be in pain, and they notice your pulled ears, not your fancy earrings. Drooping earlobes are unattractive and aging. Larger earrings should always clip or screw on. Make sure they are lightweight enough not to pull the lobe down. It is always better to buy very big earrings made from the new synthetic, extralightweight materials.

When I go to office meetings with busy TV executives who spend a lot of their time talking on the phone, I can tell immediately which ones have chosen too-heavy earrings. They're only wearing one. The other is lying on the desk.

JOAN COLLINS is one celebrity who often seems to wear big earrings that pull down her earlobes. When I ran into her in the makeup room at one TV show, I was fascinated to notice not just how very thick and dated her makeup was, but how her earlobes drooped under the weight of heavy and ornate earrings in a way that wasn't attractive, contemporary, or youthful.

⚙ **All your pearl necklaces worn layered together.** This creates a rich high-society look.

When JOAN RIVERS began hosting her television talk show, Barney's department store provided her with clothing and accessories that landed her on the best-dressed lists. Her habit of wearing multiple Chanel-inspired pearl-and-chain necklaces received so much favorable feedback from her viewers that she soon created her own line of similar jewelry for QVC, a home shopping network, and the enormous success of the line led to her own shopping show, the first of its kind on syndicated television.

✪ **A piece of velvet ribbon or raffia gift-wrap ribbon tied to the side of a long necklace.**

✪ **Inexpensive brightly painted, holiday-style wooden necklaces.** For Christmas there are jolly Santas, Christmas trees, candy canes, and minipackages; for Halloween there are pumpkins, black cats, ghosts, and goblins.

❉ **Two unexpected necklaces worn together.** Try wood beads with a brushed-gold chain. Pair a magnifying glass on a piece of cording with long pearls and a long silver filigree chain. Try black jet beads with a chain of tiny matte silver balls.

❉ **An antique watch fob as a short necklace.** I found one of these in an old shop in Israel and it has become one of my favorite necklaces. People are always commenting on how interesting and different it looks.

❉ **Art deco necklaces and earrings.** This style of twenties and thirties jewelry has seen a resurgence in the nineties. The real antiques are very expensive and hard to find, but good imitations are available at most department stores, and The 1928 Jewelry Company has built an enormous business in re-creating this delicate style from the past.

❉ **A lariat.** These thin satiny strands of cording with silver points on the ends and a sliding center clasp (also called bolos) are traditional cowboy wear, but they can look very interesting if you take them out of the Western format and wear them with a traditional white shirt or a solid-color blouse in a crisp fabric. You can slide the center up to the very top of your collar, so it looks almost like a brooch, or you can unbutton the top two buttons of your blouse and leave the slide lower and more open for a slimming effect.

❉ **Enamel jewelry.** Both necklaces and earrings can be found in this material. They are usually in bright, primary colors and are inexpensive. Enamel pieces are fun—lighthearted hearts-and-flowers images, or replicas of animals or toys. They are a very affordable gift to match to someone's personality. If the recipient loves flowers, she might get pleasure from purple pansy or red poppy earrings; if she loves cats, she might like a chain necklace of little black kittens.

❉ **Necklaces and earrings encrusted with crushed fake stone.** This method of mixing color and texture creates an effect much like that of a tweed or multihued fabric. Glued or strung together, these artful jumbled pieces of broken and chipped stone look best in pastel-quartz mixes; barely-there blues, pinks, and lilacs; warm earth tones of sand, amber, and ocher; or black-and-white, interwoven with charcoal and slate.

✪ **One or two long chains or strands of pearls crisscrossed across your chest.** Wear these chains as you would a shoulder bag, making sure the necklaces are long enough to touch your hip on one side. You can clip on charms. Donna Karan sells this look for five hundred dollars. You can duplicate the feeling for far less.

✪ **Necklaces twisted together.** By wrapping or braiding together multicolored stone strands and pearls you can create a short, thick collar, as wide as you choose, which should be worn with collarless jackets, blouses, sweaters, and dresses to create its own flattering face-framing collar. Tie the various clasps together with a complementary color of ribbon and then tie the ribbons together for your closure.

✪ **Necklaces worn backward.** Many chains and strands of beads have attractive clasps; it's a shame to hide them beneath your hair at the back of your neck. Many short chains are actually styled these days for the closing to be visible in front. Turn a chain around so the clasp can be seen in front or, if you are wearing a backless dress or a dress with a very plain back, wear a long string of pearls or a jeweled chain so that the length falls behind you.

WATCHES

One of the simplest makeovers for your watch is a new watchband. You can try it seasonally by wearing a smooth luggage-brown leather one in the summertime and changing to a black, oxblood, or deep chestnut brown skin-textured band in the winter. This easy adjustment creates a whole new feeling.

By investing in a good-quality leather band you can make an inexpensive watch look rich. The appearance value increases immediately.

If you have an old watch, you can add a Native American silver band or a thick elasticized beaded band for a casual weekend style.

If you have a small antique watch, you can make your own watch-band from velvet ribbon and tie it on your wrist to complement dressy evening wear.

WHY DON'T YOU TRY THIS WITH WATCHES?

⚙ **Plastic watches.** Buy several of these colorful, affordable watches and try stacking them all on one wrist as though they were bracelets.

✪ **Antique watches.** Don't think that just because the 1950s silver-and-diamond watch you inherited from your aunt doesn't keep accurate time it can't be used. Try wearing it as a bracelet alongside your basic watch that keeps perfect time.

✪ **Men's watches.** Try wearing one or more of these, with the strap loose like that of a bracelet, with a business suit.

✪ **Mix and match time zones.** Wear a combination of watches, setting them for different time zones so you will know what time it is if you have to make that business call to Atlanta or phone your mother in Denver.

✪ **An all-black watch.** Try this with an all-black outfit.

✪ **A tan or luggage-color leather watchband.** Try this with summer pastels, cottons, and linens. As with that luggage-color belt, you will find it works well.

✪ **A multicolored bright Swatch.** Try these whimsical patterned watches on weekends, with casual clothes and jeans.

On our first date my husband, who is a businessman, wore a typically muted conservative suit. But he had a multicolored Swatch watch on his wrist. I was immediately attracted by this touch of individuality and quickly discovered it was a true indicator of his lively fun-loving personality. No wonder I'm particularly fond of whimsical watches!

RINGS

I didn't include rings in my list of essential accessories because they are such personal items, associated with the special anniversaries and celebrations of our lives. Of course, most of us do wear rings, and not just those usually on our left ring fingers as engagement, wedding, maternity, or anniversary symbols. So here are a few ideas for those who like lots of rings.

WHY DON'T YOU TRY THIS WITH RINGS?

❂ **The sixties look.** Back in the swinging sixties lots of people copied Ringo Starr, who wore rings on all his fingers. Now, with the revival of the flower-child, peace-symbol fashions, the look is back. You can even wear a ring on your thumb, as Julia Roberts does, and toe rings can look attractive peeking through summer sandals, provided you have pretty feet and straight toes.

❂ **Men's rings as charms.** Maybe we don't all have a husband or boyfriend who won the Super Bowl or the World Series, but most men have school and college rings and if they don't like to wear them they may let you thread them on a long chain or necklace.

I wear a baby ring and my husband's college ring on a long, gold-tone necklace. I looked everywhere for the perfect chain and eventually found it in a hardware store. It's a pull chain for a toilet! I've now also added a miniature typewriter, which my father gave me because I love to write, and a circle pin from the news station where I worked in Los Angeles. I'm often asked about this unique necklace, which was originally created because I wanted a long chain on which to wear my husband's ring.

❂ **Napkin rings.** Antique napkin rings or even modern wood or Lucite versions can also look eye-catching hung on a heavy, long chain.

BRACELETS

I love mixing, matching, and layering bracelets. I always feel that several together make a more stylish statement. It's better to layer one arm and leave the other bare. You can layer bracelets on the same arm as your watch, going either for the minimal approach with a delicate link bracelet or the bold look with a heavy link or a glittery, frankly-fake bangle. But remember, jangling and clanking bracelets can be very annoying and inconvenient, both for yourself and those you work with.

I really became aware of this when I started to work in television

news and had to use a hand-held microphone. I found that the clanking and clattering created on the audio could ruin an interview.

WHY DON'T YOU TRY THIS WITH BRACELETS?

❂ **Necklaces as bracelets.** Lots of long necklaces work very well as bracelets, wrapped around your wrist for a multi-strand look. I was intrigued by a woman who clearly used bracelets as her style statement. She was wearing several and they were all obviously antique. One was an etched bangle, one a gold chain with small precious stones, another was a woven antique gold chain adorned with small tassels. The chain bracelet was wrapped around her wrist twice; it was actually a necklace. She explained that each morning her husband would tie it around her wrist. It sounds like a lot of trouble to go to, but it was obviously worth it. I'm sure I wasn't the only one to notice how creative and original her bracelets looked.

✪ **Charm bracelets.** Charm bracelets are an interesting way to record and tell the story of your life. They have everlasting popularity and can be passed on from generation to generation. You can buy charm bracelets that are already complete and have a theme—Western, toys, animals, hearts—or you can create your own by collecting charms as you experience life. You can put together an individual charm bracelet by hanging your locket or favorite charm on a gold chain bracelet, and you can wear several of these bracelets together instead of just wearing all your charms on one bracelet. You can also take an old locket and tie it on your wrist with a piece of cording or lace and make your own Victorian-style charm bracelet.

✪ **Jade bracelets.** These oriental-style bangles of stone and gold always look very elegant. They seem expensive because of the artistic way the gold is worked around the stone. Even the cheapest copies look good, but you always have to take care when wearing them because they do tend to break easily. Because of their fragile nature it's better to wear them in the evening than at work.

✪ **A mix of bracelets.** Eclectic styling is in vogue in all phases of furniture and fashion. The barriers can be removed as you try your own one-of-a-kind combinations. The only rule is that you adore the way the unexpected work together.

✪ **Good jewelry with junk.** You can mix a fourteen-karat gold chain with a pounded silver cuff. Or alternate dime-store enamel bracelets with gold bangles. Try mixing Lucite beading with diamonds. Weathered-wood bracelets complement hammered brass or pewter.

⊙ **Cuffs and snake bracelets.** I love cuff bracelets for dressing up a plain outfit for evening. You can wear a wide one alone or lots of thinner ones together. Usually they look best kept to the lower arm, but if you like to wear bracelets on your upper arm, remember that they only look good if you are tall and slender. Superfit, buffed biceps or droopy upper arms aren't the place for a snake bracelet.

Older women should always beware of exposing their upper arms, and bringing attention to them with too much jewelry.

At the 1993 Emmy Awards show MARY TYLER MOORE had everyone wondering why she had selected a sleeveless evening dress. She was wearing beautiful, probably real, diamond bracelets, but even they couldn't detract from the sight of her flabby upper arms. We all love Mary, but an evening dress with sleeves would have had the crowd at the Pasadena Civic Auditorium admiring her still-slender figure, rather than gossiping about how much-too-skinny she looked.

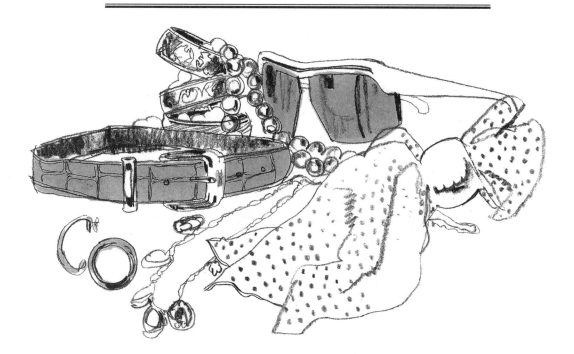

5

Scarves, Pocket Squares, and Ties to Wear Your Own Way

SCARVES

YOU PROBABLY already have many scarves. They are one of the most affordable, versatile, and colorful accessories. Scarves need never be thrown out, unless, of course, they are very badly torn or stained. Once you buy one you'll probably keep it forever. Scarves can always be recycled, since individual scarves never go out of style; it's the ways of wearing them that change with the times. This can sometimes be confusing. A multitude of diagrams, pamphlets, and how-to tapes have been assembled to teach you how to use scarves in creative ways. I find these illustrations usually just frustrate the wearer.

I use two simple methods of learning to tie scarves.

The first is to refer to your magazine clippings. When you see a scarf look you like, tear it out and, with the picture as a reference, stand in front of the mirror and practice creating that look. Try it with all the different scarves in your wardrobe. Diagrams usually suggest you have to have a specific size and shape scarf for each look, but that's often not true. You can create the look you are after with many different scarves. If your scarf is a little short, you can always tuck in the ends and secure them with tiny gold safety pins. If it's too long, an extra wrap around the neck, or just rolling and tucking the ends, can take up the extra length.

The second way is to lay the entire outfit you plan to wear on your bed, placing the accessories appropriately, so you can view the whole effect objectively. Then you can practice folding and tying the scarf different ways, placing it against the outfit each time to consider which style looks best. This really works because by removing yourself from the outfit, you get a clear picture of whether the scarf looks best twisted, folded, tucked, or hanging free.

Pretty HALLE BERRY seems to have a knack for tying scarves perfectly. She likes to wear a long chiffon scarf tied tight around her neck with the ends flowing free, a much more individual expression than the standard little square scarf tied in a triangle. She will often team the flowing scarf with a baseball cap, worn at a sideways angle, probably a tip of the hat to her husband, David Justice of the Atlanta Braves.

According to designers' whims, the scarf as an accessory goes in and out of fashion. According to women across America, they will always wear scarves, regardless of "what's hot" and "what's not" lists. You can tell if this is an "in" year by the size of the scarf selection in your favorite department store. Sometimes scarves occupy a huge area; other years they are hidden in a small corner.

When you buy a scarf think about the outfit you plan to wear it with. How much of the scarf will show? Fold it the way you are going to wear it and look at the pattern as it will be seen to make sure the colors and design will be attractively revealed. On display in the store, scarves are usually folded to show off as much of the pattern as possible, but this may not be the result when folded the way you plan. If you don't try your own method of folding while in the store, you may be disappointed at how the scarf looks when you get it home and try it with the planned outfit.

Scarves should complement an outfit—for example, a solid, rich chocolate-brown chiffon for an unadorned camel suit, or a bold purple-and-pink floral pattern to brighten up a pale lavender dress. A metallic scarf can take neutral-color summer linens and make them more festive. A delicate ivory lace scarf can lend a romantic touch to a stark, severely cut navy or black suit.

Different tying methods have come and gone. The nineties is about smaller amounts of scarf showing, particularly if the print is boldly patterned or dramatic. Gone are the big triangles over the shoulders of blazers. Today scarves are either tucked in, neat, and controlled, or freely flowing oversized oblongs in soft fabrics such as chiffon, gauze, sheer cotton, and airy silk.

With today's uneven hemlines for blouses and jackets, an oblong scarf peeking out of the hem is a very contemporary statement.

The *Today* show's KATIE COURIC is the A.M. talk-show host I find the easiest on the eyes early in the morning. She loves scarves and wears them well with the blazers and structured jackets that are almost uniforms for TV hostesses and news anchors. She wears scarves at least two or three times a week—for instance, one day a leopard-print scarf at the neckline of a camel-color shawl-collared jacket, another time a multicolored pastel scarf at the neck of a soft yellow blazer. She tucks the scarves into her jackets or twists them around her neck or ties them as ascots, so that they frame her face with just a small amount of warmth and color. This breaks the oversuited look, and it's sophisticated, not cutesy. She never looks confined by or uncomfortable with how she's dressed and therefore she's relaxed, a mood that then overflows to those she's interviewing.

WHY DON'T YOU TRY THIS WITH SCARVES?

✪ **A linen dish towel.** If you wash it in very hot water several times to soften the fabric, it works well as a scarf. You can tuck it into the neck of a high-collared blouse, sweater, or jacket, or tie it loosely. For a longer scarf you can sew two of these towels together.

✪ **A big, square scarf tied as a pareo.** Wear it belted over tights or leggings. This is a very popular look that creates the impression of a skirt. It was derived from the resort-wear fashion of tying a big square scarf over a bathing suit as a cover-up. Today's designers show the pareo worn with a traditional blazer as an innovative fashion statement.

✪ **The wrinkled look.** This is very fashionable. You can easily create your own version. Wet an oblong scarf, fold it in pleats, and tie it with string to hold it in place. Let it dry naturally in the sun. Untie and discover the wrinkled look!

✪ **A sarong.** A forty-five- to fifty-four-inch square of airy, thin, soft fabric like chiffon, handkerchief linen, fine cotton, silk, or gauze works best as a sarong. Pull the scarf open, wrap it around you, crisscross the two ends in the front, and tie them just above the bustline. This look works over bathing suits and exercise or sports bras worn with leggings. For small-busted women a twenty-seven-inch square, folded in thirds and knotted in the center, works as a bandeau top for shorts or a bikini top.

✪ **Alternative styling ideas.** Scarves can stand in for other items of clothing—belts, hats, outerwear, skirts—or transform an item of clothing for an entirely fresh feeling. An artist's look can be created by tying a long oblong scarf into a huge, soft, floppy bow at the neck of a big smock-type shirt or blouse. Fans of the Western look can use fringed scarves tied in triangles around their necks or waists. Paisley cravats can suggest a high-society, aristocratic look when tied high on the neck and tucked into sweaters or blouses. Evening drama can be created almost magically by using shimmering beaded or rhinestone-studded scarves.

✪ **Crisscrossing two scarves together.** Braided this way, scarves can be worn around the neck or as belts. Old bits of thin, frayed cotton rags can even be twisted and knotted together for a poor-boy look and worn as a belt or kerchief. They can also be twisted around damp curls to make Shirley Temple–style rag curls.

✪ **Head wraps.** For bad hair days you can take a twenty-four- or thirty-six-inch square, fold it in a triangle, place it low on the forehead (right above the eyebrows), and knot it in the back with all the ends tucked in. To that you can add a small twelve-inch square rolled on the diagonal and tied on top of the other to suggest a hat. This is a good time to use pattern on pattern, just making sure the patterns have color in common.

✪ **Antiquing.** Use tea to dye a white-and-cream scarf so it has that softer, old look. (See the instructions for dying fabric flowers in Chapter Four.) You can also use soy sauce as a dye to create a darker and richer sepia tone, but wash the scarf thoroughly after the dye has dried so you don't smell like a Chinese meal.

✪ **Bleach to soften overbright colors.** Steep a cotton scarf in a mix of bleach and water to create a weathered, sunbleached, broken-color effect.

✪ **Warm clothing.** Scarves are great stand-ins for jackets or cover-ups and they also add a layer of warmth, color, and interest over a cape, coat, or suit: try a huge fringed shawl, a lightweight Navajo-patterned blanket, or a striking light-wool clansman tartan blanket swung over both shoulders and pinned in place with a clan pin or big brooch. Make over your winter coat with a wraparound cashmere or wool muffler. Try a man's poncho as a raincoat alternative.

Keeping Your Scarf in Place

Here's a fashion tip to remember if you are wearing a button-up jacket with no blouse underneath, but with a scarf tucked in around the jacket collar. Pull the ends of the scarf through the center of your bra. This will secure the scarf and stop it from bunching up around your neck.

POCKET SQUARES

This is an idea we have borrowed from men. It's a very affordable way to add a little panache to any outfit. Unlike men you don't have to be conservative in the colors, fabrics, and patterns you put in your pocket. Since such a small amount of fabric is on show, you can afford to take real chances with your selections.

WHY DON'T YOU TRY THIS WITH POCKET SQUARES?

✪ **Personal messages.** As with many of your other accessories, pocket squares are a subtle way to display your tastes and interests. Better a floral pocket square than a gaudy floral blouse. The pocket square is less expensive and won't wear out its welcome as quickly as the blouse.

If you like stripes you might find you look ten pounds heavier in a striped skirt, but you'll merely look smart if you choose a striped pocket square.

If you've just enjoyed a trip to Disneyland, a Mickey Mouse pocket square is a much more appropriate reminder of the good time than a huge T-shirt with Goofy on it or a baseball cap with Minnie's ears.

✪ **Unusual fabrics.** Don't just stick to traditional handkerchief fabrics like lawn and cotton. All types of fabric add interesting touches to your outfit, as do all varieties of color and pattern.

✪ **Polka dots.** Spotted fabric looks attractive tucked into a herringbone, checked, or tweed jacket pocket.

✪ **Flowered prints.** A pretty contrast is to wear this with a man-tailored suit.

✪ **Gold, silver, or bronze metallics.**

✪ **White, beige, or black lace.** These delicate fabrics soften a severely cut coat.

✪ **A bold, bright print.** This will liven up a muted-color outfit.

✪ **Soft, flowery pastel chiffon.** This instantly creates a spring or summer feeling.

○ **A piece of a traditional bandana.** This provides a casual cowgirl touch.

○ **A strong, solid chocolate brown with a black suit.** With a brown purse and brown shoes this creates a very expensive look.

○ **A piece of black-and-white, or blue-and-white, linen dish towel.** This is an attractive choice with a summer outfit. As with the bandana above, cut a sizable corner from the dish towel. If you sew, hem it, otherwise tuck the cut edge into the pocket.

○ **A piece of old linen or an antique lace doily.**

○ **A thin oblong in a soft fabric.** This should be placed in the pocket so that more of the material hangs out.

○ **A spray-starched square.** This will stand up for a stiff, clean, crisp look.

⚙ **Two squares together.** Try two bright colors such as red and purple with a black jacket; two shades of camel with a beige jacket; one striped and one with small dots, both the same color; one white cotton man's handkerchief with a neutral color—black, bone, or navy—in the pocket of a blazer.

Keeping Your Pocket Square in Place

If you are worried about these squares falling out of your pockets, here's a handy tip. Buy a corsage pin at a florist's shop and fasten the square from the pocket's inside, or use a pretty antique hat pin through the outside of the pocket. You can, of course, use an ordinary safety pin. But only on the inside!

TIES

Some years back Diane Keaton as Annie Hall showed us how attractive men's ties could look on a woman, and the current success of designer Nicole Miller's fancy, cartoonish pop-art ties has reminded us that they are not just for men. Again, this is a much subtler way of signaling your tastes and interests than a slogan T-shirt or an overall homage to a theme.

I've had one tie for seven years, and it's my favorite. It's black with big white polka dots. It's a man's tie. Michael Gelman, the producer of *Live With Regis and Kathie Lee,* has the same tie, and it's one of his favorites. I wear mine with a strand of pearls over it. Gelman doesn't!

I love to decorate ties to create a theme, not just for myself but also for some of the men I know. One Christmas, when I'd done a "Decorating for Holiday Dresses" feature on TV, I sprinkled a tie with charms—a miniature Christmas light, a candy cane, a tiny Santa, a little TV set, a wee microphone, and a crown—and presented Regis Philbin (the king of morning television) with this gift.

I've created baby shower theme ties—adorned with safety pins, plastic toy babies, miniature baby food tins, and bottles and wooden initials for the baby's name—which have been hits with the fathers who now often attend baby showers along with their wives.

You can buy these ornaments at miniatures shops or hobby and craft stores. Use your fabric glue or glue gun to attach them to ties.

WHY DON'T YOU TRY THIS WITH TIES?

⊙ **Your own theme tie.** Take any number of your favorite pins with similar characteristics or buy amusing miniatures, toy or gift-store decorations and create your own decorated tie.

⊙ **Tie your tie differently.** An alternative way to wear a tie is to tie it and then unbutton the second button of your blouse or shirt and tuck the tie in. Then button up again. Only the knot and a couple of inches of tie are showing. It's a boy's prep school look that is surprisingly flattering and fun on women.

6

Belts, Bags, and Gloves in Addition to the Essentials

ONCE YOU HAVE your essentials you are ready to add some wonderful options. In leather, quality is important. When buying belts, bags, and gloves, you should always go to the full extent of your budget. They will not only last for years but actually improve with time.

BELTS

My husband and I both have to attend many black-tie events in connection with our work. Yet I haven't bought any new black-tie outfits for years, relying instead on a combination of mix-and-match black separates—long and short skirts, black silk pants, vests and blazers in satin and velvet—which I wear with a variety of intriguing accessories.

I often use belts to alter and adorn my outfits, as I did when I wore four belts with my black tuxedo pants and a black turtleneck body suit to the Academy Awards show. I chose a black suede belt with a gold buckle, a gold chain, a black-and-gold Chanel-inspired chain, and a pearl-and-gold chain. I threaded the black suede through the belt loops, then I strung the three chains slightly lower around my hips. I clipped them together with a small black-and-gold quilted coin purse.

That was my outfit. It wasn't expensive, but it made an eye-catching statement even amid all the celebrities in their expensive designer gowns

(whether their own or just on loan for the night from stores like Fred Hayman in Beverly Hills). Quite a few people stopped to ask me how I had created my Chanel-style waistline.

Evening clothes worn without accessories look unfinished. Remember JULIA ROBERTS attending the Oscars show a few years ago in that dun-colored gown? It was an Armani dress, and it's hard to go wrong with Armani, but she hadn't bothered to have it fitted to her figure and she hadn't selected any accessories to enliven its dull color. So her appearance was a big disappointment to everyone who expected better taste for the *Pretty Woman* star. In contrast, ANNETTE BENING looked beautiful at the Oscars. She was also wearing a simple Armani gown but the dark blue color was much more appropriate under the bright lights, it fitted perfectly, and it was accessorized ideally with long navy gloves, pearl-and-diamond earrings, and a matching bracelet. She looked memorable in the right way.

Other suggestions to dress up your evening wear are gold, pewter, or bronze waist rope belts and colorful faux-gem-bejeweled chain belts or show-stopping sparkling rhinestone belts.

WHY DON'T YOU TRY THIS WITH BELTS?

⚉ **More than one.** Try mixing and matching. It can work for both day and evening. The belts must have something in common, whether size, style, color, or texture.

Gold and black work well together, as do gold and pearl, but if you decide on gold and silver make sure you continue the theme by mixing your jewelry in the same way.

For casual wear, especially with jeans, you can mix denim with Lucite, or with men's colored belts.

A wide cummerbund can be secured with a thinner rope, a thin belt, a satin curtain cord, a strip of rolled fabric, or a rolled scarf.

The unique silver belt buckles from designers Elsa Peretti and Barry Kieselstein Cord are an investment item, but you increase your investment by buying their colored and textured interchangeable straps to create a variety of looks.

❂ **Fifties elastic belts.** These cinch belts never completely disappeared, but lately have made a real comeback owing to the popularity of sports-inspired street wear. Exercise enthusiasts like to put a long loose skirt over a leotard and add a cinch belt at the waist. Katey Sagal, the star of TV's *Married . . . With Children,* is fond of this look, on and off the screen. I recommend elasticized cinch belts only if you have a very small waist and a very flat stomach; otherwise they add pounds and draw attention to figure flaws that looser belts can camouflage.

❂ **Purse belts.** Designers like Donna Karan and Calvin Klein have sold this look for at least four hundred dollars, but you can easily create your own by hooking a small brown- or black-leather coin purse to a brown or black belt. The purses cost only about ten dollars. A shoemaker can easily attach a hook to the purse for you or you can clip the two elements together with one of those double-ended keychains. I have often created this look on my makeover segments and it's been a big hit with both the participants and the TV audiences.

❂ **A watch-fob chain or a short, eight- to ten-inch, chain.** Either a real watch fob or a piece of lookalike chain can be hung from a belt, or the chain can be looped from the belt into a pocket on the trousers. Once you have the right length drape to the chain, pin the end inside your pocket with a safety pin.

A modern variation on this idea is one of my personal favorites: Donna Karan's three-inch-wide olive-brown leather belt with a wide antique brass buckle and dangling chain on which you can clip one or more of her charms—a leaf, a book, a cross, or a coin. You can create your own version of this by clipping one or more pendant necklaces to your belt.

❂ **Ethnic belts.** Obi sashes from Japan work well as wide cummerbunds, tied with a large flat bow in the back and worn with an all-black

bodysuit or a tuxedo outfit. Native American conch belts with silver and turquoise strung together or spaced along a leather thong work well with linens, cottons, and denims. Moroccan silver or gold coins or hammered chains suit long, full, festive Mexican or Indian gauze skirts, crinkled cotton dresses, or black bodysuits. A multicolored Swiss embroidered cotton belt can enhance any plain casual dress or blue jeans. Caribbean pirate belts of very wide leather, with square, bold buckles suit tiered skirts and T-shirts, oversized shirts, and leggings, or a bodysuit.

◉ **A man's tie.** Use a man's tie as a belt with denims or khakis or solid-color slacks.

BAGS: WHY DON'T YOU TRY THIS WITH BAGS?

If you choose to go beyond the essentials, here are a few suggestions.

◉ **Very small shoulder bags worn crisscrossed.** You can mix and match colors—bone, taupe, black, navy, red—wearing several together as you would long chains.

◉ **A leather clutch with removable shoulder straps.** This works for both day, with a strap, and evening, as a clutch.

◉ **Old purses.** You can find these in thrift shops and at garage sales in expensive areas of town. You'll discover that they are usually of very good quality, and good leather only gets better over the years if it is properly cared for. They can be polished up with saddle soap or a car paste wax, or, for a few dollars, at a shoe repair shop. There's more to look for than just traditional women's handbags. Old doctor's bags and small dressing cases, fashionable in Victorian times, can make interesting purses even today.

◉ **A scarf purse.** A twenty-four- to thirty-six-inch square of beautiful fabric, tied corner to corner hobo style, will make a wonderful evening purse.

◎ **Copycat designs.** Some copies of traditional styles by Chanel, Bottega Veneta, and Prada are attractive and affordable. They may not last as long as the real thing, but at rock-bottom prices you can afford to replace them.

◎ **Large sports totes or sailcloth, canvas nylon, or oilskin duffel bags with drawstring closures.** These are all made in new lightweight, high-tech, sturdy fabrics, and allow you to carry more than a traditional big tote.

◎ **Carpet bags, whether the real thing (made from Persian rugs) or re-created in rich thick tapestry.** This is another attractive style of large bag that can be used as a tote or an overnight or travel bag.

◎ **Canvas and leather backpacks.** These used to be just for hikers, but they've become a very popular mainstream fashion for casual wear. They have the advantage of leaving your hands free and distributing the weight of heavy items across both shoulders.

◎ **Attaché cases.** For the career woman, large envelope shapes and traditional attaché cases can hold all your business paraphernalia as well as your personal items. Many have shoulder straps as well as handles. The most traditional and practical colors are black, brown, and oxblood.

◎ **Patchwork colors.** If you wear a lot of solid bright colors you might try a bag with many patchwork colored shapes. It will blend in with and pick up on whatever color you are wearing, eliminating the need to change your bag constantly.

GLOVES

Once you've purchased the essential gloves, you might want to create a more varied and exciting glove wardrobe. Gloves are the absolute finishing touch. I always think of wearing gloves well as the ultimate in accessory chic.

WHY DON'T YOU TRY THIS WITH GLOVES?

☺ **Short white or ecru cotton or kid gloves.** This is a pretty style for summer, worn with linen or heavy cotton suits, or sleeveless print dresses.

JULIA ROBERTS, in the hit movie *Pretty Woman*, wore this type of gloves with a sleeveless, full-skirted, belted brown polka-dot dress and a big hat, to turn all heads at the polo match.

☺ **Pigskin, cowhide, lamb's-wool, or cashmere wrist-length or slightly longer gloves.** For winter, wear gloves like this to work, crushed or rolled down into cuffs, with all your heavy coats, bulky sweaters, and thick shawls. Bright colors like teal, red, or purple will give your winter coat a midseason pick-me-up.

☺ **Short, tight-fitting, cut-out driving gloves.** You don't have to be a professional driver to wear these. They go well with sports clothes.

☺ **Fingerless gloves.** These are fashionable again. There are black ones for evening, so you don't have to remove your gloves to use your knife and fork.

☺ **Thick, woolly, fleece-lined leather fingerless gloves.** This is a sporty, rugged look.

You can also make your own knit pair from worn-out woolen gloves by snipping off the fingers and stitching the ends with a contrasting color of yarn.

7

Stockings and Shoes for More Options

ALTHOUGH, as I've explained, it's not necessary to have a vast shoe wardrobe, most of us love to buy shoes. Even if we're not sure what they will go with, an interesting and unusual pair of shoes often tempts us to spend our money. With luck we will get lots of wear from our shoe choices. We are certainly more likely to do that if we think of imaginative ways to coordinate them with stockings. You can get more style for your dollar from stockings than any other accessory. A five-dollar pair of panty hose can virtually change the whole feeling of an outfit.

STOCKINGS AND SOCKS: WHY DON'T YOU TRY THIS WITH STOCKINGS AND SOCKS?

❁ **Polka dots.** Try these under herringbone or tweed man-tailored slacks.

❁ **Thin stripes.** Try single-color striped hose—white on white, bone on bone, gray on gray, black on black—under solid-color or small-check pants.

❁ **Opaque camel or café-au-lait.** Try these under white linen pants or white or beige linen skirts for summer. The plus to wearing these colors, rather than white, is that there will be no visible pantyline—often a problem with too-light sheer stockings under light or white clothing.

○ **Textured checks, herringbone, or triangles.** Try these under tweed or herringbone slacks for a texture-on-texture, opposite-pattern look.

○ **Jewel tones.** Try emerald green, cobalt blue, or ruby red under an all-black pantsuit in which the vest or blouse is also black. This is a much more sophisticated look than wearing a jewel-color blouse.

○ **Navy-and-white stripes.** Try these under blue jeans when you are wearing them with a white T-shirt.

○ **Rhinestones.** Try these decorated hose under black pajama pants, but don't wear them with a dress.

○ **Holiday themes.**
For Christmas try red or green tartan plaid under red, black, green, gray, or navy slacks.
For Halloween try bright orange opaques under black slacks.
For New Year's Eve try silver, gold, or bronze under black or ivory slacks.
For Valentine's Day try white opaque with hearts or red dots under black, red, or white slacks.

○ **White cotton short socks or knee-highs.** These look sporty with everything from tennis shoes and loafers to ballet flats. Pair them with khaki slacks and a white shirt to suggest a weekend in the Hamptons.

○ **Scrunched-down white cotton sport socks.** Scrunch these above lace-up boots or high-top tennis shoes. This is now seen as a mainstream fashion look, especially when worn with skirts of all lengths or wide-legged pants.

○ **Thigh-high black opaques.** The modern version of the garter belt look, held up with elastic tops. What was once considered bad girl nylons, these are now shown worn with short skirts or walking shorts by the classic and conservative designer Ralph Lauren.

❂ **Woolly knitted leg warmers.** Once just professional dancers' work gear, these have long moved from the confines of the dance studio to become casual sporty wear when worn over tights, with tennis shoes or boots.

❂ **Argyle or cable-knit socks.** Worn with moccasins or flat lace-up shoes, they make a nice addition to the tailored look.

❂ **Footless cotton tights.** In white or ivory, under long or sheer summer skirts, these are a good summer alternative to white opaque stockings. They should be worn with a completely flat shoe.

❂ **Fishnet panty hose in black or white.** These wide-mesh stockings are a flashback to the sixties. If you have fantastic legs they look great with short skirts, but only if the outfit is tailored and low-key; otherwise the look is too trashy.

SEAN YOUNG seems to like fishnet tights, worn with open-neck blouses and tight spandex skirts. It's one of the very obvious choices she makes in trying to draw attention to herself. She plays with her jewelry and wears clunky shoes, which allow her to talk about her passion for tap dancing or leap to her feet to demonstrate her moves without much prompting. She's actually got a beautiful face and a slim, elegant figure and would probably be considered a classic beauty if she cut her hair simply, wore smarter clothes and simple accessories, and chucked away that fishnet legwear!

SHOES: WHY DON'T YOU TRY THIS WITH SHOES?

You will never lack for footwear once you have acquired the shoes on the essentials list. But new shoes, like a new fragrance or shade of lipstick, are always a great pick-me-up purchase.

❂ **Small ankle boots.** They can be dressy lace-up leather, worn with scrunched-down socks, almost hidden under long skirts and dresses. I wear this look sometimes. Once, when I appeared this way on *Live With Regis and Kathie Lee*, Kathie Lee, who has basic, traditional taste when it comes to shoes, looked down at my feet and commented bluntly, "You have to be very confident to wear that kind of shoe." Several years later I noticed she selected the same look to wear with long flowing skirts and dresses for her at-home wear.

Rugged outdoor-style canvas boots or crepe-sole suede boots look good with wide-legged cotton or linen walking shorts or, alternatively, with old-fashioned flowered dresses.

LAUREN HUTTON likes this style of active-wear boots. She still works the high-fashion runways although she is over fifty, as appealing a model as she ever was when she was the superstar face and figure of the seventies. She has stayed attractive because she always favors the clean-cut look, whether it's from J. Crew or Calvin Klein, and has used accessories sparingly, often favoring the classics. I noticed her in neutral, natural-color linen slacks with a plain white shirt. With this outfit she was wearing a burlap-and-leather backpack and army-green, fatigue-style high-top tennis shoes that had black rubber toes and resembled boots. These were trendy touches, but worn this way, the accessories looked classic and appropriate, the right accents to set off a simple outfit.

❂ **Riding boots.** These can be traditional English or Western style. English riding boots look wonderful with trousers or with tights tucked into them, worn with a traditional blazer, white shirt, and an ascot at the throat for a riding-to-hounds look.

Western or cowboy boots are probably, year in and year out, the most popular boot. I recommend buying ones with just a small amount of top stitching so you can wear them with outfits other than blue jeans.

❂ **Motorcycle boots.** This is a craze I feel is best left to bikers, but if you really must have a pair, then wear them with a plain black pantsuit or blue jeans.

Extreme styles in boots tend to look better on younger women. DIANA ROSS's appearance in thigh-high shiny vinyl boots just didn't look right. Many newspapers and magazines criticized her choice. Perhaps TINA TURNER, though she's actually older than Diana, might have got away with this bold, funky look, but Diana didn't. Even younger stars make this mistake. I saw MEG RYAN at a Hollywood movie screening. She was wearing combat boots with a short black dress and a choker ornamented with a cross. All three of these items were hot at the time, but to wear them all was overkill.

❂ **High-heeled shoes with straps, whether T-bar or instep strap.** These are traditional dance shoes from the twenties, when the energetic Charleston hit the heights. They may fade from the fashion magazines, but they never entirely disappear for the women who like a delicate shoe. Because they are so feminine they should always be worn with skirts, whatever length or shape, rather than trousers.

❂ **Ballet flats.** One of Chanel's most popular shoe styles is its two-tone ballet flat. You can find many more affordable versions. Like black patent Mary Janes, they look good with delicate, feminine dresses and, in the summer, walking-short suits. Wrap the thick fabric laces around your ankles, or if you have great legs lace them crisscrossed up to your knees.

❂ **Rope- and crepe-soled canvas espadrilles.** These are choices for casual wear. You can buy them in platform style or flats.

⊙ **Colored tennis shoes.** A pair of bright red tennis shoes can really spark up your weekend blue denim look.

Celebrities like CYBILL SHEPHERD and DAVID LETTERMAN have popularized the idea of wearing these casual athletic shoes with business clothes and formal wear. They can not only afford lots of pairs, they can also afford to be considered slightly eccentric. Now these shoes come in so many different styles and colors it's easier to make them work with many of your outfits. If you do a lot of walking or suffer from sore feet you can still look stylish in comfortable tennis shoes. For example, boot-style, two-tone high-tops in a burlap fabric can be as smart as and more comfortable than an ankle boot.

When I sat near CONNIE CHUNG on a plane, I noticed, much to my surprise, that she was wearing tennis shoes with her traditional business-style outfit. She looked as well-turned-out as she always does.

⊙ **Strappy leather sandals.** In low or flat heels they are the perfect casual shoe if you have attractive, well-manicured feet; otherwise rely on your essential flats.

⊙ **Spectator pumps.** In black and white, tan and white, or navy and white, these are attractive for dressier daytime outfits.

⊙ **Bordeaux or oxblood.** These deep, deep reds work as an alternative to black or brown shoes.

⊙ **Suede in neutral colors.** This has become acceptable year-round.

❁ **Moccasins.** These can take the place of tennis shoes with your blue jeans, khakis, or walking shorts.

❁ **Lace-up brogues.** These walking-style shoes are punch patterned, with cut leather fringes or tassels. They provide a wonderful balance to pantsuits.

❁ **Loafers.** Whether you wear them with socks or panty hose, with traditional pennies in the toes or in patent leather, they are always comfortable and thus always popular.

❁ **Metallics.** Gold, pewter, and bronze, preferably in a subdued matte finish, can be used as neutrals. They work with most summer clothing, whatever color or fabric, and are another choice for a dressy evening shoe.

❁ **Tuxedo loafers.** They can be bought with or without insignia, in patent or suede.

❁ **A brocade.** In a slip-on or low square heel this is a rich, Renaissance look.

I recommend staying away from shoes with large appliqué or gilt detail. Ornamented shoes draw too much attention to your feet, which throws off the balance of your overall appearance. I much prefer to see extra details close to your face.

I warn people to stay away from strappy high heels for evening, unless the straps are wide and supportive. After an evening of cocktail chatter or dancing, your feet swell and overflow your shoes in a way that is not only uncomfortable but unattractive.

8

Hats, the Forgotten Accessory

I ADORE HATS, but these days they have become the forgotten accessory. People have worn hats since ancient times, not just for warmth but as fashion statements. In this century, until the late fifties, women rarely went anywhere without a hat.

A hat was considered an essential part of an outfit and some of our most striking images of the great movie stars, from JOAN CRAWFORD to GRETA GARBO, show them wearing hats. On screen and off, these two screen goddesses appeared over the years in many high-fashion varieties of hat, but essentially each favored a very different style. Crawford, who was aggressively up-front about being sexy and glamorous, wore big picture hats, almost like aureoles around her dark hair, while Garbo, whose allure was much more mysterious, wore tight-fitting cloches or fedoras pulled low on her brow.

Recently there's been a trend in modern movies to show stars wearing hats, but these attempts have had as little impact as the movies themselves. I think this is because everyone, even the most confident star, is a little intimidated by hats.

Whenever I'm in a department store I notice women trying on hats. They glance around self-consciously to see if anyone is watching them and if they do catch anyone looking, they quickly remove the hat and give up on the idea of trying to find one that suits them. Because they haven't grown up surrounded by women wearing hats they don't know how to wear them or what to wear them with.

But now that hats are no longer expected, they are probably our strongest, most dramatic accessory. That's the reason I love them.

PRINCESS DIANA has done a great deal to popularize the wearing of hats among younger women, but I don't think she really feels comfortable in many of the hats she chooses. The English royal tradition demands she wear them for formal occasions, but often she looks outwitted by her headgear. She's clearly more comfortable when she wears something like a baseball cap with her casual clothes. However, her formal hats are often dramatic and beautiful, but worn to best effect in neutral tones rather than bright colors for daytime.

Here's How to Capitalize on Wearing a Hat.

◉ **Make sure you are in the right frame of mind.** You do need to feel confident on the days you wear a hat because it will draw extra attention to you.

◉ **Make sure you are having a good face day.** We all have days when, for one reason or another, we appear more or less attractive when we look in the mirror in the morning. Pick a good day to try wearing that hat.

◉ **Don't worry if you are having a bad hair day.** Bad hair days are actually perfect days to wear a hat because you don't need or even want a hairstyle when you wear a hat.

An elaborate hairstyle detracts from a hat and vice versa. Your hair can be pulled back very plainly or tucked up when you are wearing a hat. Make sure you won't have to take your hat off at any time during the event you are attending. Remember that it's not wise to wear too big a hat if you are attending a sports event, or are at the movies or the theater, because you'll annoy the people behind you.

◉ **Wear your hat pulled on firmly.** Your hat should frame your face, not balance on top of your head, so pull it on properly; don't be tentative about it. Low in front, right over the eyebrows, is usually the most flattering and practical look.

☼ **Make up your face very carefully.** As the hat will draw attention to your face, make sure you take a bit of extra time with your cosmetics. You can perhaps be a bit bolder with your makeup because the hat will balance the effect. Try an extra dusting of matte powder.

☼ **Start with the hat.** When you decide to wear a hat, don't add it to the outfit you've already chosen. Begin by choosing the hat you want to wear and then build the outfit and accessories around it.

☼ **Keep your above-the-collarbone jewelry small.** Remember, the hat itself is the statement; don't lessen the impact with oversized earrings and chunky necklaces.

☼ **Don't feel you have to match the color of your hat to the color of your outfit.** A contrast in color and texture is usually best. Neutral hats are the most practical.

The GABOR sisters, EVA and ZSA ZSA, may still wear yellow hats with yellow dresses, shoes, and bags but that color coordination is both contrived and old-fashioned.

☼ **Don't match your hat shape to your face shape.** If you are round faced stay away from circular hats such as derbies and bowlers, which will just make your face look fuller.

If your face is angular veer toward softer hats and avoid high brims and sharp angles, which look harsh.

DEMI MOORE, who has a round face, looks best in off-kilter, angular hats, which wouldn't suit someone like, say, Anjelica Huston, who has strong, sharply etched features.

✪ **Check the mirror both close up and full length.** To make sure the hat you like suits your face, stand very close to the mirror and check it from all angles, including both sides and the back. Then step back so that you can see yourself full length to tell whether the hat works well with your body proportions.

You'll be delighted to find how a hat can modernize your look, make you appear slimmer by drawing attention away from your body to your face, make you stand out from a crowd, and earn you compliments. If the hat is interesting it's natural that people will want to see who's under it.

I remember being drawn by the sight of a very beautiful antique flowered straw hat at one movie industry party. Despite the other distractions of good food, amusing speeches, and the sight of many stars, I had to find out who was wearing the hat. I worked my away across the crowded room to see. It was a very pregnant KATE CAPSHAW on the arm of Steven Spielberg. The hat was worn with a retro dress, little ankle boots, and scrunchy socks.

There are, of course, all sorts of hats. Here's a rundown of the most popular:

✪ **Baseball hats.** A very popular look in the last few years, a baseball hat is still the ideal weekend wear. Teamed with amusing sunglasses, it's my favorite choice, especially if I haven't had time to wash my hair. And remember, if you color your hair, as so many of us do, it really is an easy way to protect it from the sun.

Real baseball caps are best left to men. You may be a big fan of the Phillies or the Braves, but their logo caps are not cut to suit women; they have a squarer line and the top tends to stand up in a way that looks unattractive. If you must wear one then don't buy the cheap kind. Get the ones the real players wear, which are more rounded, made of wool, and sized correctly.

Smaller, more curved baseball caps in softer fabrics designed espe-

RIGHT

WRONG

cially for women are available now in most department and specialty stores. They are a much better choice.

Despite its being a hot trend, baseball caps worn backward don't even look good on men, so I don't recommend you wear them that way either.

✪ **Scrunch hats or "crushers."** I really like these hats, which can come in any fabric from burlap to rain-treated cotton to evening velvet.

They are easy to travel with because they take up no space and don't crush.

They don't press hard on your head, so they don't become uncomfortable or prevent you from resurrecting your hairstyle easily when you take them off.

The three-inch brim allows for additional accessorizing so you can use an attractive pin to flip up the front or back for a variety of different looks, which will let the hat take you from day to evening.

✪ **Berets.** A beret really places the emphasis on your face. Again, this is a very easy hat to travel with because it can be rolled up and slipped into a pocket. It's also useful to have on hand if the weather turns wet and windy.

Berets usually look best worn very low on the forehead in the traditional beatnik style, which itself was copied from French workers. If you are very petite you might want to stuff the crown with tissue or a scarf to give more height because a flat head makes you appear shorter.

Since berets are usually plain, you can quickly and easily add your own accessories: A rhinestone pin or a silver or gold ribbon bow gives an instant evening look. A striped ribbon adds a schoolgirl touch. A velvet ribbon in a contrasting color—purple on blue perhaps—makes the whole appearance dressier.

JACKIE ONASSIS liked wearing a beret. On the thirtieth anniversary of President Kennedy's assassination she wore a plain beret with her dark sunglasses and a long dark coat when the paparazzi caught up with her as she walked through Manhattan to meet friends and family.

☉ **Tams.** A tam, or tam-o'-shanter, is a smaller, more structured version of the beret, usually topped with a pompom. The structure makes it a little less easy to wear.

Remember how good MARY TYLER MOORE used to look in one on her TV show, and how she used to toss her tam up in the air in the show's opening credits?

☉ **Cowboy hats.** Whether in felt or straw, these hats look flattering on most people. But be warned: they look much better worn in contrast to a romantic long skirt or a sleek bodysuit than with a complete denim outfit and cowboy boots.

☉ **Retro hats.** Cloches, the hats worn by 1920's flappers, are soft, crowned "bells" with a small brim that sometimes drops over one eye. They can be unadorned or festooned with ribbons and flowers.

COWBOY HATS

FEDORA

CHER, who is not usually someone I would point to as a fashion example, actually used a cowboy hat well once at an awards show taping. She paired a ribbon- and flower-strewn hat with a modest, plain pantsuit rather than one of her better-known ultrarevealing, glitzy outfits.

STRAW HATS

FELT HAT

BOWLER

BERETS

Straw boaters, à la *Gigi,* derive from the uniform of French and English schoolchildren.

Fedoras are the man's-style hats like that worn by Ingrid Bergman in *Casablanca.*

Big picture hats, like those that always looked so stunning on Audrey Hepburn, are best for weddings or special occasions such as the Kentucky Derby or Ascot. They are so dramatic they need a special event to make them appropriate.

Little pillboxes were popularized by Jackie Onassis when she was Jacqueline Kennedy.

Any hat that reminds you of times past is a retro hat, but that doesn't mean it can't be worn today. A sleek modern outfit often looks wonderful with an old-style hat.

Some of Hollywood's young stars are really catching on to this look, particularly TV's Mayim Bialik of *Blossom.*

✪ **Straw hats.** Straw hats are particularly flattering to the face. They come in all shades, from light hay and pale wheat to darker tans and cocoas.

They are very easy to adorn with flowers, lace, and ribbons or a combination of all three accessories.

They can also be worn in a sportier way, like scaled-down cowboy hats, when wrapped with a scarf or bandana.

HILLARY RODHAM CLINTON got mixed reviews at the inauguration when she wore that formal blue hat with her checked suit, but when she wore a straw hat during her Martha's Vineyard vacation she looked so great that stores across the country were quickly sold out of this type of hat.

✪ **Men's hats.** The fedora is really a man's style; back in the 1940s few men went out without wearing one. Men's departments and old clothing stores are a good source for finding one in a small enough size. Rather than wear it with a severe menswear-style outfit, try one with a

PICTURE HATS

long-skirted suit. Feminine touches can be added—a cameo pin, for instance, or a lace band with a flower pin.

✪ **Felt hats.** Felt is a popular fabric for all hat shapes. The texture often works well if you match the color of your hat to your outfit, especially with dark and muted hues such as blacks, grays, browns, burgundies, and forest greens. I still feel that if you favor a bright color, you should wear it in contrast to your ensemble; don't try for a match.

Felt is an easy fabric to handle, and you'll find it simple to pin on accessories.

At an elegant party I took a simple, small-brimmed black felt hat and added some veil netting sprinkled with tiny rhinestones and some gold and black velvet ribbons. I tied this strip of netting into a bow and pinned it to the back of the hat so that the filmy trails hung down my shoulders. Then I tied the gold and black velvet ribbons around the hatband. This created an ultradressy look to wear with my basic-black separates—a bodysuit and a long skirt—and it didn't entail any complicated

sewing, just tying and pinning. The decoration could be easily removed so that next time I could wear my felt hat plain with jeans. I received lots of compliments, especially from men, who seem to love hats on women. They didn't realize I had created my hat with extremely affordable trimmings from my local fabric store.

✪ **Schoolboy-style caps.** These are small and neat with a round crown, often with some type of emblem above the narrow visor.

◎ **Urchin-style caps.** These have a baggier crown and a larger brim and are perfect to tuck your hair under on a bad hair day. In windy weather try tying a long square or oblong scarf over the top of this style of hat to hold it on. As an alternative, a wide ribbon might also work well to keep it secure.

◎ **Soft knitted caps.** These pull way down over your ears and are perfect wear for cold, windy weather. To make them look fashionable rather than utilitarian, try pinning a spring flower to the front or side.

◎ **Tweed caps.** This is a man's style that looks attractive with informal country clothes and vests, hacking jackets, and jodhpurs.

◎ **Sailor's cotton or canvas caps.** These caps, which are usually trimmed with nautical insignia and white rope or gold braid, can look very chic if worn with simple dark blazers and slacks, rather than teamed with a full nautical outfit.

CAROL CHANNING, bless her heart, is a real nautical victim in her favorite sailor look with white bell-bottoms, a gold-trimmed cap, and captain's jacket. She could take lessons from both RALPH LAUREN and DONNA KARAN in how to make the nautical look tasteful. So could Donna Karan's friend and client BARBRA STREISAND, whose choice of this type of hat, when she showed up to cheer on tennis pro Andre Agassi at Wimbledon, seemed inappropriate. A pretty straw panama would have looked much more charming in this traditional English setting.

◎ **Black velvet hard hats.** The de rigueur English-style fox hunting cap can be attractive when teamed with tweedy clothes or black slacks, white shirt, and black boots, but it's a hard-edged style that is not extremely comfortable and is usually better left to the horse show ring where it really belongs.

HAIR ORNAMENTS

Though some women may never try wearing a hat, at one time or another almost everyone feels a need for a hair ornament or some other accessory to control and improve her hairstyle. Hillary Rodham Clinton was the object of criticism and the subject of jokes because of her headbands, but clearly she isn't someone who wants to spend a lot of time on her appearance. When her hair was long, a headband was a practical solution, and in hindsight the many hairstyle changes she has gone through show this was not a bad look for her after all.

All hair ornaments were designed to keep our hair pinned up, pulled back, clipped off our face, or gathered up away from our shoulders, but recently they've moved from the merely practical to the truly fashionable. Now you can find headbands, barrettes, and clips that are covered with all types of fabric from casual rope-type canvas and chintz prints to elaborate velvet and gold. The rubber band has given way to the covered ponytail holder, which is now decorated with flowers, shells, and beads. This no longer costs pennies but can run to over twenty dollars.

If you love barrettes or combs, the most practical is the traditional tortoiseshell, but you can really help a bad hair day by adding decorative styles. If you are creative you can apply your craft skills and use your glue gun to attach little shells from the beach, tiny straw and fabric flowers, beading and glitter, and even bits of broken stones from old jewelry to decorate your own barrettes, headbands, and ponytail holders.

9

Eyeglasses, the Often Necessary Accessory

MANY PEOPLE who wear glasses don't think of them as an accessory, but as a necessity. If you are an eyeglass wearer, I feel they are your most important accessory because of the many options available today in shape, color, and style. Dorothy Parker's "Men seldom make passes at girls who wear glasses" simply isn't an appropriate quip anymore, because glasses can actually enhance your appearance.

According to the National Eye Institute, 60 percent of all Americans now wear eyeglasses, so obviously we feel more comfortable and attractive in them than we used to or we'd all be struggling with contact lenses.

READING GLASSES

If you own only one pair then follow these basic accessories rules:

❂ **Stick to the conservative.** Don't buy anything with a fancy trim or a lens tint. The simpler the better.

❂ **Stand back from the mirror** as well as up close when selecting your glasses. You want your glasses to blend in with your hair color, brow shape, cheekbones, and whole appearance, not jump out as a spectacle.

❂ **Consider the specific area around your eyes** rather than the shape of your whole face. The glasses don't have to be round or square just because your face is that shape. Your bone structure will determine the best pair for you if you follow these guidelines:

• The top of your frame should be the same shape as your eyebrows.

RIGHT

WRONG

- The top of the frame should cover your brows. Anything lower or higher will confuse people, as you will look like you have a twin set of brows.
- The bottom of the frame should hit your cheekbones.
- Frame width should align with your temples. Wider or narrower frames fight your natural bone structure.
- The bridge of the glasses should be light in color unless your eyes are very far apart. Dark, double, or ornamented bridges only accentuate close-together eyes, while clear bridges open up the distance between them.
- The thickness of the frames should conform to your bone structure. It has nothing to do with height or weight. If you are small boned, choose a more delicate frame. If you are large boned, select a wider, heavier frame.

❂ **Choose a color that blends with your coloring.** When you are looking in the mirror, shove the glasses up into your hair. If they blend in with or are lighter than your hair color you are on the right track. Cary Grant may have got away with wearing dark eye frames even after his hair turned gray, but most of us can't. We don't want frames darker than our hair because then people notice our glasses before they see us.

❂ **Think of your lipstick color.** If you look best in pink then you will want cooler colors; if you favor oranges or reds you will want warmer tones.

If you have silver, gray, ash blond, neutral brown, or black hair you will look best in silver metal frames or plastic tortoiseshell that are flecked with gray and cool, ashy browns.

If you have golden blond, warm brown, auburn, or red hair you will look best in gold metal frames or plastic tortoiseshell flecked with warm yellows and bronzy browns.

Pale pastels, pink, gray, blue, lavender, straw, or wheat-color frames look good on most people.

If you wear glasses all the time and your budget will allow you to own several pairs, you can also afford to go beyond these basic rules and use your glasses as you would any other whimsical accessory, to denote a change in mood or style. Like anything else eyeglasses can be found at bargain prices, whether through sales, at antique stores, or in bargain outlets.

By popping out the lenses of affordable sunglasses you can replace them with your reading prescription. Find a friendly, willing optician or optometrist since they make a large profit on the mark-up in frames. But a frame is a frame and you can really save.

Remember that because you may not be wearing your new prescription and your eyes may still be dilated from the optical exam, it can be hard to see when you are choosing frames. You will be particularly vulnerable to the advice of opticians' clerks. They are not always the best people to offer this advice. They are usually pushing the trendy and the expensive, and oversized, star-shaped, hot pink lenses are unlikely to be a wise choice. There was a period a couple of years ago when they were promoting photo-gray tinted lenses, which were meant to work as sunglasses as well. A lot of people fell for this look only to find that the glasses were unattractive, the gray reflection was not flattering to any skin tone, and the lenses were not dark enough to be used as sunglasses either. Luckily, we don't see them worn much anymore.

Don't be talked into fads, but don't totally shy away from trying something different. My sister Susan is an attorney who has to dress for work very conservatively, but she's found she can add amusing touches by wearing a whole different variety of glasses that reflect her outgoing personality.

For those days when you feel you need a little camouflage, lightly colored tinted lenses can look very pretty. Lavender and soft blues and greens are flattering colors to hide tired puffy eyes. It's better to put on a pair of tinted lenses than to do a rush job on your eye makeup. It's also better to be wearing those tinted lenses than to be seen with no eye makeup, because you never know who you may bump into even in the supermarket.

Hot-color frames can look fine if you have the strong personality to match.

Wearing glasses even if you don't need to can sometimes be a useful makeover. If you are very youthful looking, I've found that glasses can help to give confidence and credibility during a job interview or business meeting. I once put distinguished wire frames on a young minister to help him make a serious impression when delivering his sermons.

SALLY JESSY RAPHAEL's now-signature red glasses happened by accident when Burt DuBrow, producer of her talk show, which originated in St. Louis, suggested she needed a distinguishing look for the show's first taping. An intern sent to the local eyeglass stand returned with red frames, which have become her trademark. When a promotional party was held for her at the Beverly Hills restaurant Maple Drive, all the waiters wore knockoffs of her famous red specs! She is careful not to wear any other accessories that vie too boldly with these glasses. She's fond of wearing a simple cream suit with just small earrings and no other jewelry.

GLORIA STEINEM is famous for her big aviator-style glasses. She's scaled them down over the years, but even though she's finally cut her hair short, she's still keeping to the same shape in eyewear. They are her signature.

ELTON JOHN, of course, became known for his glasses, which ranged from the conservative and the traditional to the huge and outlandish, and dark thick frames were no impediment to stardom when it came to the late rocker BUDDY HOLLY.

Surprisingly for such a beautiful woman, SOPHIA LOREN doesn't wear glasses very successfully, even though she is promoting her own line. She always seems to pick a very homely style although her exceptional face structure could use something either simpler or more avant-garde. DARYL HANNAH, who is also very beautiful, isn't very smart in her choice of eyewear either. She favors thick, nerdy frames, which don't flatter her blond-goddess looks.

Another time I realized I'd made a mistake when I tried to bring youth to an older man by adding modern, small wire frames to his updated clothes and newly colored hair. These old-fashioned granny-style glasses, which have recently become so popular made this older man look like a grandfather!

A look I never recommend is half-glasses. I think they make everyone look ten years older. A lot of the high-powered male and female executives who've consulted me about their appearance insist they need them when making speeches so that they can look at their notes or read a TelePrompTer while still seeing their audience clearly. They don't want to be seen in full glasses—even though these days bifocals can be perfectly blended—so they are convinced the half-glasses are better. I always insist that they'll look younger and more professional in full glasses.

You can wear your glasses attractively even when you are not wearing them to see. Instead of putting them down where you probably won't be able to find them when you want them, you can keep them with you by wearing them various places:

WRONG

RIGHT

• On top of your head as an impromptu headband.
• Tucked into your belt.
• Tucked into the top of your shirt.
• Tucked into your breast pocket with one ear piece dangling out.
• Hung around your neck on an eyeglass leash. (You can buy these in eyeglass stores or, more affordably, make them yourself. Leashes used to be thought fuddy-duddy, but now look rather attractive if you think of the cord in necklace terms.)
• Shoulder-strap case. These faux or real leather cases for reading- or sunglasses are worn crisscross as you'd wear a minipurse. They are found in the purse departments of most larger stores.

SUNGLASSES

Sunglasses are an excellent way to have a bit of whimsical fun.

We don't really perceive them as part of our whole appearance. We associate them with glamour because the way celebrities wear them has always been very influential—think of what Tom Cruise did for Ray Bans by wearing them with his underwear in the film *Risky Business* or of the lasting style Jackie Onassis established by wearing huge dark glasses. From the era of Lana Turner to that of today's glamour girls like Virginia Madsen, hiding behind dark glasses in the hope of not being recognized has been an attention-getting star trick.

Despite this celebrity image, most of us feel comfortable wearing sunglasses, because we can remove them at a moment's notice. However, the more we wear them, the more we must take them seriously and consider their size, shape, and style as we would those of regular glasses. Any and all of the following are wonderful to own.

WHY DON'T YOU TRY THIS WITH SUNGLASSES?

❂ **Small Oliver Peoples–style** rounded or oval wire frames with your business look.

❂ **Sleek all-black frames and lenses** for a sophisticated look.

❂ **Light tortoiseshell** or pale-pastel translucent frames with your summer whites and linens.

❂ **Brightly colored plastic** frames with neutral-color clothing.

❂ **Oversized wraparounds.** These protect your eyes and skin, particularly if you are spending a day at the beach or out on a boat.

❂ **Wearing them on the brim of your baseball cap** once the sun goes down.

Don't try mirrored lenses. It drives people crazy to try to talk to you while seeing their reflection bounce back at them.

10

Accessorizing the Basic Black Dress for Any Occasion

AT LEAST ONCE A YEAR I put together a TV segment on the many ways you can wear the basics in your wardrobe. This segment is always a crowd pleaser because it gives new ideas about how to revitalize pieces of clothing you've had for a long time and want to keep wearing.

My first advice is to make sure your wardrobe contains certain classic standbys. I am surprised how few women's closets, whatever their owners' budgets, contain the items that I feel are must-haves. These basic items of clothing are essential for a number of reasons.

They can be worn over and over. They can be mixed together to form various looks. They cut down on your packing when you travel. They can be accessorized to look correct for professional, casual, or evening wear.

The clothes I feel are must-haves are:

✿ **A black suit.** This is the number-one outfit to own. I find I can often travel successfully taking just this suit and a pair of blue jeans. If it's a pantsuit it works with tennis shoes and T-shirt. If you add a white shirt, vest, and tie it takes on a serious mood for daytime activities. Buttoned all the way up and belted, or worn with a silk or lace camisole and rhinestone jewelry, it dresses up for night. This is the time to stretch your budget and buy the best you can afford. One that comes with both a skirt and pants is a great investment.

❂ **A neutral-color skirted suit.** Choose banker's gray, tan, or navy or one of the new-style neutrals, which include olive, taupe, and stone. This takes you from work to business meetings to evening engagements when worn with a white blouse or white shell top. If you pair it with a white T-shirt or denim shirt it becomes casual. The jacket of the suit mixes with khakis, blue jeans, or a neutral-color dress.

❂ **Khaki trousers.** These were invented to hide dirt, and that remains one of their most valuable qualities. They are the Ivy League staple that David Letterman wore every night with a blazer before he moved up into the world of expensive suits. You can wear them successfully with a blazer. More casually, you can tuck them into boots and wear them with a white shirt or layer on a cardigan, buttoned or belted, under your black suit jacket or your navy blazer. Or you can be informal by rolling up the legs of the trousers and adding a white T-shirt and sandals.

❂ **A navy blazer.** This blazer goes over both your jeans and your khaki pants, as well as over sweatpants and leggings. It can also be worn with a wide variety of skirts and pants. It is the essential jacket.

❂ **Blue jeans.** Who can live without them? I recommend not wearing them tight. The easy, looser fit is more comfortable and also more figure flattering. Most women I have worked with are obsessed with their size, but since no one sees the size label inside your clothing, let the fit dictate your choice and forget about the number. Almost every shirt, blouse, sweater, T-shirt, and vest in your closet goes with this essential.

❂ **A denim shirt.** This handsome, practical, and flattering colored shirt is one of the best unisex looks. Pair it with blue jeans for an all-denim look or wear it under your black or neutral-color suits. You can also wear it over a white T-shirt or tied at the waist on top of a tank top.

⚙ **A white cotton T-shirt.** Buy them by the dozen. They are a contemporary alternative to blouses. Always buy one size up to allow for shrinkage, and open the package to feel the fabric and check for thicker cotton, which is the quality you should choose. The thin ones look cheap and are too sheer for wearing without your jacket.

⚙ **A white blouse.** Take a hint from the men and buy a classic white oversized cotton long-sleeved shirt. Choose small pointed collars, which can be worn up or down. This is such a versatile item in your closet because it works with almost everything—as a cover-up for a swimsuit or coordinating with either khakis or blue jeans, or with your daytime suits, both neutral and black. This type of shirt is so clean in its styling that it really begs to be accessorized.

⚙ **A black dress.** This is the one essential garment we have always heard a wardrobe must have. It's really true. It will become your best friend. It's your fall-back position whenever you are in doubt as to what to wear. Styles and price tags will vary. I feel it is best to choose the plainest long-sleeved, round-necked straight chemise—no defined waistline—you can find. By avoiding a collar and a defined waist, you are free to use more accessories in many more fabulous ways, as I will show you. Choose a lightweight fabric—fine wool, cotton, silk, or a non-shiny synthetic. This will work for you all year round and from day to evening. Try to stretch your budget to buy the best you can afford. Watch for sales because once you own this essential black dress you'll never want it to wear out.

By the clever use of accessories you can create almost any look you might need. Doubtful? Well, just look at these numerous ways you can accessorize a basic-black dress. Many of these ideas will also work well with your other must-have basics.

WHY DON'T YOU TRY THIS WITH YOUR BASIC BLACK DRESS?

1. Add black leggings, either solid or ribbed. A wide leather or suede belt in a neutral or bright color goes around the waist, while a gold or silver chain belt is dropped lower, with the dress pulled up slightly to blouson at the waist. (The best way to create the right proportion of blouson is to raise your hands above your head.) For jewelry, wear big drop earrings and two large cuff bracelets on one arm in a metal that matches the chain belt or a colored enamel that blends with the suede or leather belt.

✺

2. Wear a tan beret. Natural wood beads, incorporating shades of cream, sand, camel, walnut, and cocoa, should be wrapped around as a short necklace. Around one arm stack multiple sizes and shapes of bracelets in similar woodsy tones. Pick up the tan theme with patterned or solid opaque stockings. Add short, heeled boots in black or brown leather or suede.

✺

3. Under your dress wear a black turtleneck bodysuit and black opaque stockings. Drape over one shoulder a big, plaid blanket shawl and secure it with a wide belt that picks up one of the colors of the shawl—red, gold, green or blue, for instance. Wear large, but not drop, earrings in a matte, metal, or coordinating ruby, amber, emerald, or sapphire stone color. High—almost to the knee—black leather or suede boots complete this outfit.

4. A man-tailored black or charcoal pinstripe blazer goes over a white buttoned-up, pocketed vest. Ornamentation is provided by a gold or silver watch fob going from one vest pocket to the buttonhole. Wear sheer black nylons with black pumps in suede, leather, or patent.

✪

5. This is a schoolboy look that is created with a white, pointed-collar cotton shirt worn over the dress. The shirt has French cuffs, with cuff links in metal (shiny or antiqued), stone, or inexpensive fabric colors; find them in the men's department of your local store. Over the top of the dress put a double-breasted black vest into which is tucked a black-and-white polka-dot tie with only the knot showing. Sheer black stockings and pumps are the final touch.

✪

6. A white full-bodied poet-style shirt is worn with the collar turned up. It is buttoned, except for the top two buttons, which are left open to reveal the neckline of the black dress. A long, oblong floral chiffon, cotton, or lace scarf is tied loosely around the neck, hanging down like a long tie. A white or neutral-color soft fabric hat is worn with a turned-up brim and a flower pinned to the front or side, holding the brim in place. Choose nude nylons and black or taupe heels.

7. This is a weekend look. A denim shirt is tied at the waist over the black dress, with the sleeves of the shirt rolled up. Tied layers of chunky chain necklaces, in any shining metallic color, lie in the hollow of the neck. A white, denim, black, or gray jockey cap is worn with large sunglasses. Black opaque footless leggings are worn with white canvas tennis shoes.

❋

8. This is a business or professional look that starts with a banker's gray blazer in flannel or wool, buttoned all the way up. A printed scarf in an abstract design, using gray or black combined with another color, is tucked into the neckline. A black, gray, or luggage-colored leather belt is worn over the blazer. Gray opaque ribbed stockings are matched with mid-heel lace-up shoes in any of the essential colors.

❋

9. This is a variation on the uneven hemline style. A long white blouse is worn buttoned up over the black dress, with a cream or ecru scarf tied as an ascot and held in place by the dress neckline and a tie pin. A short, black, buttoned vest creates the exposed shirttail look. Black tights go with flat dark-color riding boots. Additional accessories are short white cotton gloves and an oversized man's watch worn over the cuff of the blouse.

7

8

9

10. This is a soft romantic look, created with a long, sleeveless, embroidered or patterned tunic vest in a soft, flowing, drapey fabric. It is worn open, with the additions of a small leather belt decorated with charms, large hoop earrings that match the charms, opaque black tights, and flat black slip-on shoes.

❂

11. This is a feminine twist on the menswear look. A white oversized man's cotton shirt, with the sleeves rolled up, is blousoned over a black belt at the waist. A black bow tie is worn with three strands of long necklaces—all stones or beads, or a combination—mixed in with chains. Black sheer nylons and black medium-high heels are the finishing touch.

❂

12. A fitted, flared, waist-defining, buttoned-up jacket, in any solid color of neutral or bold bright, goes over the dress. The jewelry consists of large gem earrings, which complement or match the jacket color, and two or three gem lapel pins, one a stickpin and one that matches the jacket. This time the nylons are nude and the pumps match the jacket color.

13. This is a bad-weather outfit. A ribbed turtleneck sweater, in any color, is worn under the black dress. A felt Annie Hall–style hat goes with round glasses. The dress is belted with a long black or oxblood leather belt tied at the waist. A long black raincoat, with the belt tied at the back, goes over all this, worn with black ribbed or textured tights and black or oxblood boots. You can create this style in all black or shades of gray, or you can select a color or other neutral for just the turtleneck and the hat.

❂

14. A wide-collar, ribbed-cotton turtleneck is worn under the dress, with sleek black stirrup pants that turn the dress into a tunic. A medium-wide leather belt in black or brown is added, along with textured white or neutral socks with flat loafers. An additional accessory is a long cord or chain, perhaps bought from the hardware store, with sunglasses or eyeglasses attached.

❂

15. A white cotton crewneck T-shirt is worn under the dress. A soft, plaid flannel lumberjack-style shirt is layered on top of the dress and left unbuttoned. Over the shirt goes a shorter neutral-color blazer with the sleeves rolled up. Sporting accessories are a bandana at the neck, picking up a color from the plaid shirt, a rugged, woven leather belt with a large brass buckle, and a baseball hat in black or a color that complements the bandana or the shirt. Heavily textured neutral-color leggings are worn with crepe-soled loafers.

13

14

15

16. This is a vacation look. A plaid or print pareo (a big square cotton or linen scarf that is also used as a swimsuit cover-up) is wrapped around the waist with the slit to one side. It is cinched in place with a medium-width leather or elasticized belt. Scrunch the sleeves of the dress up to the elbows and add several large bangles and the ethnic earrings of your choice. Keep your legs bare and wear low-heeled sandals.

✿

17. A three-quarter-length buttoned vest in wool, in a bright color, is ornamented with a soft flower pin at the neckline. A pocket watch and chain are tucked in the vest pockets. Stylish sunglasses, charcoal or black tights, and flat black leather or suede shoes complete this more feminine professional look.

✿

18. This is a variation on the Parisian artist's look. A lightweight camel or oatmeal round-necked sweater is worn under the dress. Tan stirrup or slim-leg pants are tucked into brown ankle-length lace-up boots. A tan leather or suede belt at the waist blousons the dress. A camel, sand, walnut, or cocoa sweater is tied around the shoulders. Drape a gold chain necklace from the belt.

16

17

18

19. A silver concha belt in black, red, or luggage-colored leather is worn with a neutral-color cowboy hat. A faded red or black bandana is rolled and twisted diagonally and tied at the neck. Large silver hoop earrings are the jewelry. Red cowboy boots are worn over thick black tights.

❀

20. This is a romantic look that is flattering to fuller figures. An oversized linen blazer in a barely-there neutral color is accessorized with a cream or ecru lace pocket square held in place with an antique pin. Add a natural-color straw hat, with flowers pinned to the turned-up brim, small antique or filigree earrings, and a crocheted or tapestry shoulder bag worn across the chest. Linen or taupe leather heels go with nude nylons.

21. A winter coat in black, burgundy, or any other rich dark color is teamed with a matching fedora. A long oblong shawl, in a light or bright color, is tied around the neck and draped over the shoulder. Wear leather gloves in black or the color of the shawl, any earrings from our essentials list, and any black, high, winterized boots.

❂

22. This is a weekend active-wear look. A short olive-drab army vest with multiple pockets is worn over the dress, which is belted with a wide cotton-web belt in black or shades of olive. Wear an elasticized head-band, trendy sunglasses, and a wide leather bracelet or other wrist wrapping in black or olive. Thick white socks are scrunched over lace-up desert boots with thick crepe or rubber soles in dark tan or near-black olive.

21

22

23. A white long-sleeved, V-necked, oversized sweater is tied at the waist with a man's striped or foulard tie. A short pearl necklace and earrings are the jewelry. Nude nylons go with low black heels.

❂

24. A cream or off-white tailored blouse is tucked into your panty hose under the dress. A double-breasted or shawl-collared tweed or textured blazer, in either black and gray or camel and brown, is worn over the dress. The blazer is belted in a wide luggage brown or black. The professional details are a hair bow in any neutral shade to hold your hair back, small tortoiseshell glasses, a briefcase, nude or taupe nylons, and classic low-heeled leather shoes.

❂

25. For evening wear, a black silk or chiffon floor-dusting robe with side or back slits is worn over the dress, which is belted with a shiny gold or rhinestone belt. Bold rhinestone or gold earrings and black gloves, scrunched down with bracelets worn over them, are the very festive touches. Sheer black nylons go with black heels.

23

24

25

26. Gold epaulets made from ribbon are attached with stitching or pins to the shoulders of the dress to turn it into evening wear. A long, sheer, sparkling gold scarf is pinned through one epaulet. Big earrings are in gold, Lucite, or jet beads. Black sheer stockings are worn with black pumps, decorated with shiny or jeweled clips.

❂

27. A wide velvet ribbon is used as a belt with rhinestone pins clustered at the front and the bow tied in back. Big rhinestones also clip on the ears, and an oversized scrunchy velvet beret is worn low over one eye. Sheer black nylons are teamed with black pumps with rhinestone clips attached.

❂

28. A small felt pin-trimmed hat is worn at an angle. Three black-and-gold chains with a small purse attached layer around the waist. Wear short black gloves with a wide cuff bracelet in black or gold on one wrist to match the belt and small jet or gold earrings. Sheer black nylons are matched to black pumps.

26

27

28

29. A high-buttoned white vest goes over the dress underneath a white double-breasted tuxedo jacket. Several antique or flower pins are arranged down the lapel. A chain-and-mesh purse with a long strap is worn across the jacket. Delicate black or gold earrings and sheer black nylons with black pumps are the additional accessories.

❂

30. A sparkling, beaded gold, silver, or bronze scarf in a soft fabric is tied as an ascot and tucked into the dress. Earrings match the metallic color of the scarf. A small evening shoulder bag is worn with black sheer stockings and black heels.

❂

31. A cream, flowery, or lace patterned scarf is worn around the neck of the dress. A thin, unadorned black belt goes around the waist. An organza cream flower is pinned in the hair. Small pearl earrings go with pearls, which are wrapped choker style around the neck. Sheer black stockings are worn with black high heels.

29

30

31

11

How to Use Accessories to Take Off Pounds

WHETHER YOU LIVE in Los Angeles, the toned-body capital of the world, or in the Midwest, where good old-fashioned home cooking is still in favor, the pressure to be slim is so intense you probably wish that you looked a little thinner.

Women are obsessed with their weight, often needlessly.

According to *Consumer Reports* magazine, three million dollars was spent by Americans in 1992 on diets. Many of the people who try these weight-reducing programs do need to lose pounds. While working on their diets, though, they can learn to hide those extra pounds with clever dressing and the use of appropriate accessories.

I'm not suggesting you stop working out and eating wisely, even if you are only slightly overweight. I'm just showing you a less painful way to look as though you've lost a few pounds.

I'm not someone who believes all those fashion editors who tell big women that these days anything goes and they can wear whatever they like, however bold the print or bright the color. I'm sure that advice is well intended, but I believe that careless dressing only draws more attention to how big you are.

My philosophy is quite different. I think it's fine to use zingy prints and flashy colors in your accessories but, if you are heavy, the basic tone from head to toe should be a muted color.

Here are my suggested fashion rules:

AVOID LINE BREAKS

This is my most important rule.

Let me explain what a line break is: It's any division of color or detail that breaks up the line of your body.

An extreme example would be a woman in a red jacket, with a white belt, a blue skirt, white stockings, and red shoes. That would make four line breaks, and the woman in this outfit would look shorter, boxier, and heavier than she actually is.

The eye stops each time it confronts a line break; the image is jarring, the effect unattractive.

This doesn't mean you are condemned to a life of monochrome uniforms. One or two line breaks are fine.

For instance, a navy blue dress paired with navy or dark stockings and shoes can be accessorized with a belt with, perhaps, a bold, geometric silver buckle or, alternatively, with a striking red belt. This makes just one, very effective line break.

When you are dressing in a hurry it's easy to overlook the line break problem. So here's a tip.

Take the entire outfit you have decided to wear and lay it out on the bed, placing the accessories appropriately—necklace and/or scarf at the neck, belt at the waist, stockings and shoes below. Stand back and consider how many times your eye is stopped by a line break.

The slimmer and taller you want to appear, the fewer times your eye should stop. Considering this before you start putting your clothes on will ultimately save you time and enable you to make changes more calmly. We all know how it feels when we see we haven't got our look right. Pressed for time, we start tossing off items and grabbing others to try on. That's always the moment when the belt gets caught in the belt loops, the knot in the scarf won't untie, the stockings snag.

It's always wise to remove at least one line break from any ensemble you choose, just as Marilyn Monroe did with her jewelry. She'd give herself a final checking over, then take off one item.

For example, if the choice is a man-tailored brown pantsuit with a white blouse, tan textured socks, and brown-and-white spectator shoes,

WRONG   **RIGHT**

*Take the entire outfit
you have decided to wear
and lay it out on the bed,
placing the accessories
appropriately.*

you would find three line breaks—at the waist, where the blouse meets the pants; at the ankle, where the pant legs meet the socks; at the shoe, where the socks meet the shoes. If you are really tall and slim that's fine, but most everyone wants to look taller and leaner. Even one fewer line break here will contribute to that effect, so find a nontextured sock, as close to the color of the pantsuit as you can, and you'll look better.

As I mentioned, four line breaks are always too many. For instance, if you take a navy multicolored flowered dress and wear it with a pink blazer, pink belt, nude nylons, and navy shoes, you've created those four line breaks—at your waist, at the hem of your blazer, at the hem of your dress, and at your shoes. It would be much better to cut out three of them by wearing a navy belt, a navy blazer, and navy stockings, so that the only line break is where the hem of your flowered dress meets your stockings. You'll appear to be two inches taller and ten to fifteen pounds slimmer if you do this.

OPRAH WINFREY's fluctuating weight makes her an interesting celebrity for larger women to study. Sometimes she gets it right, but too often I feel she has too many line breaks. Her basic outfits are well chosen, but the accessories don't follow those slimming rules. She too often draws attention to her waistline. Once I noticed she wore a brown leather belt over the defined waistline of her burnt orange blazer. A matching orange belt without an ornamental buckle would have been so much better. Another time she wore a long, soft chiffon scarf in a small blue green print with a blue dress, which made her look taller and thinner. The scarf was so long it almost reached her knees. She tied it right below her bustline, so an elongating vertical line slimmed her down. When Oprah is slim her taste is impeccable, but her use of accessories is very limited—earrings and an elegant gold watch. Because Oprah is one of the most watched and admired women in America I am always wanting to add just a few exquisite accessories to her outfits— a beautiful antique pin on a collar, a delicate chain with a special charm, an interesting solid color or printed fabric square to her jacket, or a long string of mixed textured beads to a muted dress.

DELTA BURKE also doesn't cope with her ups and downs in weight very well. She too often looks like a Liz Taylor wannabe, wearing too many glitzy accessories that are too rounded for her frame, with too-tight clothing. She likes to wear, for example, a fitted, flared hot pink jacket, ornamented down one side with black sequined pins, over a black skirt. This emphasizes her waistline. It would be much more flattering if she chose a long, loose pink jacket over a black skirt worn with black nylons and pumps and a long strand of pink beads.

PAY ATTENTION TO PROPORTION

This is another key matter to consider when using accessories so that you look slimmer and taller. Your accessories should be in proportion to your real size.

KATHY BATES is always very well turned out when she attends awards shows but she's slightly too conservative in her look. She sticks to an important fashion rule for larger women by not wearing clothes that are too tight, but she often makes the mistake of wearing small accessories. She'd look better with bigger earrings or a larger purse.

CAROLE SIMPSON, the ABC news correspondent who anchored the political "town hall" meeting during the last presidential race, dresses very well for a larger woman and understands proportion. She never wears jewelry that is too small or insignificant. I saw her in person at the American Women in Radio and Television convention dinner. She was wearing a black suit with striking rhinestone jewelry. Her earrings were large but didn't dangle, so she looked elegant and professional.

- Tiny jewelry and small, delicate scarves make large people look larger.
- Huge jewelry and big scarves make small people look smaller.

It may seem picky to throw any criticism in the direction of CBS news anchor CONNIE CHUNG, whose look is meticulously sleek, but I do often feel that she makes a mistake in the shape of the accessories she chooses. She goes for rounded earrings and scarves tied high at the neckline, when angular jewelry and a scarf pulled away from the neckline to form a V would probably flatter her face shape more.

MICHELLE PFEIFFER, HEATHER LOCKLEAR, and WINONA RYDER are small, fine-boned women who understand how to accessorize in correct proportion to their size. Even at the dressiest premiers Michelle never wears big, bold accessories, preferring tiny diamond post earrings. Heather selects delicate short chains to wear around her neck and additionally emphasizes her waist with narrow belts. Winona favors the kind of delicate Victorian-style jewelry she wore in *The Age of Innocence* and *Dracula* or finds modern equivalents such as a tiny cross.

Two tall young stars, BROOKE SHIELDS and LAURA DERN, know that small jewelry would be lost on them. But that doesn't mean they go for dangling, clunky items. I've shared a dressing room with Brooke, and Laura often eats at one of my favorite Los Angeles restaurants, Orso, so I can vouch for the fact that they are both more beautiful than they sometimes appear on screen. Their sense of proportion also extends to the way they match their jewelry to a variety of hairstyles. They know a bold hairstyle is set off by retro-style earrings—perhaps gold and filigree clip-ons; a smooth chignon is best shown up by colorful clip-ons such as large square ruby gemstones surrounded by matte brushed gold.

Another tall, big-boned star, KIRSTIE ALLEY, overdoes not the size but the quantity of the extravagant, whimsical jewelry she wears. Her lush hair and bold features would look better if she confined her jewelry just to her ears or her wrists, instead of wearing it every place she can.

❂ **Avoid chokers.** The fashion for chokers is causing a lot of mistakes.

Everywhere I go I see women of all shapes and sizes wearing tight ribbons ornamented with jewels around their necks. It's a pretty, romantic look, so I understand why women are attracted to it, but just because it's fashionable doesn't mean it's for everyone.

During one makeover session I had a hard time convincing one petite, but fuller-figured, woman that chokers were not for her. She had been thrilled that the outfit we had chosen, a bodysuit and flowing tunic in the same muted tone, made her look slimmer and taller, but she wanted to wear a tiny choker with it, insisting, "It's really fashionable. It will look perfect with this easy sixties-style outfit!"

She didn't get the idea that it was wrong for her, creating a stark line break, until I showed her the attractive alternative. I took a simple geo-metric gold pin and placed it above her left breast. This drew the eye and enlivened the outfit, but didn't cause any line breaks and didn't interfere with the slimmer, taller impression the outfit had created.

✪ **Avoid short necklaces.** As a rule, anyone who is full busted should shy away from even the simplest chain necklace if it lies high around the neck or only reaches the bustline. That's pointing a sign at something that probably already gets enough attention. It's much more flattering to leave the neck area open and clear. The collarbone, even on the heaviest of women, is one of the slimmest parts of the body, so to re-veal it suggests "thin" even if that's not the reality elsewhere.

○ **Wear long necklaces.** Chains, ropes of pearls and beads, and cords that hang below the bustline are much more flattering. They keep that slim collarbone area open and draw additional attention away from a large bust.

○ **Avoid big, round accessories.** If you are inclined to be heavy, avoid big, rounded shapes, which will only accentuate already rounded proportions.

Don't choose large circular earrings, round belt buckles, or circle pins.

Go for the angles. Pick geometric shapes—triangular earrings, oblong belt buckles, straight rectangular pins.

○ **Place jewelry off center.** Don't put pins under your chin or down the front of your blouse.

If you wear one on your shoulder, on your lapel, or on one side of your chest, it will be more attractive and draw the eye away from your figure faults.

○ **Avoid tight ascots and bows at the neck.** The same rules apply to the use of scarves as to necklaces. Tight, bunched, and high adds to the impression of heavy and short.

The actress BEA ARTHUR usually chooses flowing outfits that are flattering to her tall, large figure, but then makes the mistake of wearing scarves too tightly wound, high around her neck. If her purpose is to camouflage her neck, a long oblong scarf wrapped once, with the ends hanging down, would work. The long, flowing ends of the scarf would create a vertical line, which is slimming.

○ **Wear softly folded scarves.** Like long necklaces, scarves tied loose and falling away from the neckline create the impression of slim and tall.

✪ **Avoid wide, contrasting belts.** An over-wide, over-ornamented brightly colored belt is usually the first line break to eliminate.

Self-colored or neutral-tone belts with small buckles covered with matching fabric or leather are always more flattering.

Fuller figured women can still wear belts, but they should be inside

a jacket or cardigan sweater or a big overblouse with the sleeves rolled up, so that little more than the buckle shows. This gives waist definition without revealing the whole measurement.

A petite woman—someone under five feet four inches—will appear taller if she drapes a belt lower on the waist on a single-color outfit. If she's also a few pounds too heavy, placing the belt under the jacket, sweater, or shirt also helps.

⊗ **Wear dark, muted stockings.** Navy, charcoal, chocolate brown, deep olive, and black are always more flattering to the legs, while cream, white, pastel, red, and purple instantly add pounds.

However, if your muted one-color outfit is an unusual off-color shade—grape for instance—I think it's a mistake to try to match the color exactly. You'll look better in black, smoky gray, or taupe, or any shade that is slightly darker than your outfit. It will create a line break, but a flattering one.

⊗ **Avoid patterned stockings.** Unless you have really long, really slim legs, these always make you look shorter and heavier.

It's particularly important if you are heavy or short to follow a basic rule about stocking color. It should match the color of the hem of your trouser or skirt, continuing the downward flow, or it should match the color of your shoe, moving upward. The exception is an outfit in a very bright color, such as purple or red; with brights, you should choose taupe or a flesh color slightly darker than your own skin.

⊗ **Stick to basic shoes.** Follow the rules I suggest regarding closed toes and heels in the section on essential shoes.

Foot-revealing strappy sandals and open heels and toes, which allow the foot to spill over, are unattractive if you are heavy.

Also avoid shoes that are very delicate. If you are short, teetering on very slim high heels doesn't make you look comfortably taller, just awkward and unbalanced.

Shoes that are decorated with bows and ornaments are also to be avoided.

○ **Buy shoes a half size larger.** If you do this and then slip in a shoe pad you will find it not only more comfortable but slimming. Nothing is less slimming than a large foot squeezed into too tight a shoe.

○ **Carry large bags.** Tiny little bags create the wrong proportions. If you are large, you can handle a larger bag, for both day and evening.

○ **Tilt your hat or wear large hair ornaments.** You can wear large hats, but make sure they are worn at an off-center angle. Plunked flat and straight on your head, they create a line that is broadening.

Politician BELLA ABZUG wore hats that suited her size, and currently, singer PATTI LABELLE is a full-figured woman who understands that her extravagant hairstyles need wide headbands and bold ornaments to keep the correct proportions.

○ **Keep the hat ornamentation in proportion to the hat.** Don't put skinny little ribbons or tiny pins on your hat. Make the trim large but simple.

12

Shopping Around for the Unusual and the Best Bargains

HOWEVER MUCH money we have, most of us love a bargain.

Finding accessories at bargain prices is particularly satisfying and also allows for creativity and imagination in an area of dressing where this is appropriate.

It's fun to go to rummage sales, to hunt in the basement and notions departments of stores, to go through your aunt's attic and garage to see what you can discover to build your accessory collection.

The accessory counters of your favorite department stores are where the latest, hottest items are on display. If you want to be first with a new look, this is the traditional place to shop. It's the place where you'll probably find the accessory that caught your eye in the most recent issue of a fashion magazine—the accessory you just must have, whatever the cost.

Even if you are on a tight budget, it's a good idea to check out these stores for the latest looks. By noticing the way accessories are used on the mannequin displays, even if you have to find them at alternative shopping sites or make them yourself, you can get many ideas about how to wear the newest styles.

Here are some places to look:

FAMILY ATTICS AND GARAGES

Often we don't realize what's hidden away in our own storage areas or those of other family members.

That pin your mother wore on her first date went out of fashion, or was never worn again once she met the real man in her life. It's probably still in her jewelry box, and now it might look fashionable and interesting on you.

Cameo pins; jeweled watches, plastic bangles, and beads from the fifties; and hippie beads and flower pins from the sixties and seventies are all back in fashion. Ask if you can take a look in those old boxes your mother put in the back of the garage a few years ago. You may not find any real heirlooms, but you will probably find some amusing items that can be recycled and reworn.

My friend Vann Ferber, a television producer, was the first person to book me as a makeover expert on a talk show. She dresses conservatively, but she usually wears an eye-catching collar-length gold charm necklace. She's known for it.

Vann didn't buy it in a department store; she found it in an aunt's jewelry box. It was originally a bracelet, adorned with the charms the aunt had collected on her world travels. But Vann felt it was too important to be a bracelet on her wrist, where it would clank against things every time she moved, so she adapted it as a necklace by affixing a leather strap to make it long enough to fasten around her neck.

MEN'S DEPARTMENTS

I often find items I need, particularly belts and pocket squares, in the men's department. They are as well or better made and usually more affordable than equivalent women's items. Besides belts and scarves, this is a good place to look for watches—to be worn loose like bracelets—and knee socks to wear under pants.

Men's belts are usually made of very good leather, which will last longer for better value, and the extra length means versatility. They can be tied to fit: wrap the belt through the belt loop, buckle it, and tie it in front with the end pointing down. Any shoemaker can punch extra belt holes if you need them.

The recent fashion trend for vests has resulted in an array made specifically for women, but more economical and more varied choices have long been available in the men's department and still are.

Suspenders are also a men's item women can use as an attractive accessory, as are ties, including bow ties, which can look great with a black evening pantsuit and white blouse.

The selection of ties in the women's department is very limited. The men's department has serious, fun, outrageous, and politically correct ties. When I met President Clinton at a Democratic fund raiser he was wearing a conservative blue suit, but his brightly colored tie was covered with figures of children. It was the topic of much cocktail party conversation. Several women said they'd love to wear a tie like his.

A white piqué evening tie looks terrific on a white crisp cotton shirt for day wear.

Silky patterned or solid bow ties work very well with colored blouses in matching or contrasting colors, instead of a necklace or scarf.

Tie tacks, which can be clustered on blouse collars and coat lapels, are another accessory you can pick up while pretending to shop for the man in your life. You'll also find a much better choice of cuff links, which can upgrade the most standard blouse.

Boxer shorts, with the fly sewn up, make cute leisure or sleep wear as does the old-fashioned, long, baseball-player-style underwear that several designers have brought back into style.

You can wear this type of underwear in a very feminine way by putting it under flowery, filmy dresses—slightly unbuttoned if the dress is long, or peeking out below the hemline if the skirt is short.

I did a feature about how to wear these long johns on the *Today* show and when I sent the executive producer, Steve Friedman, a thank-you note for having me on the show, it was written on the seat of a pair of long johns. I don't know if anyone has checked yet to see if he's wearing them, note and all!

TUXEDO RENTAL STORES

Most of these rental stores sell used tuxedos at fantastically low prices. Since they are rented in so many different sizes, you can usually find components that will fit you.

A white tuxedo shirt looks great with a white or black bow tie and a black skirt and pants or even jeans.

Evening suspenders can look very dashing under your trouser suits.

Black tuxedo pants or a black tuxedo jacket mix with black separates for black-tie events. It is better to use pieces rather than wear the total look, though more and more women are adopting the whole outfit for dressy events. I was at a party where the beautiful model Paulina Porizkova wore an entire tuxedo outfit with enormous rhinestone earrings. Smashing! Princess Diana has also been seen in her version of black tie, worn with some of the crown jewels.

JUNIOR AND TEEN DEPARTMENTS

Even if you are not a junior or a teen you can find both good items and good value in this area of the department store. You'll know you are in the right place when the background music suddenly changes from mellow tones to noisy top-forty hits. These departments display the most up-to-date looks at the most economical prices.

If you're old enough to have already owned a fifties poodle skirt, a sixties patchwork coat, or seventies bell-bottoms, then it probably isn't wise to wear them now that they have come back into fashion.

Remember, if you have worn a look when it was first in fashion, you don't wear it again this time around. That doesn't mean you can't pick up on the accessories of eras past that have also returned. The junior department is probably the easiest and least expensive place at the moment to find silver crosses on cord chains, flowery pins and earrings, crocheted purses, vibrant flowered and psychedelic-print socks and leggings, and kooky scrunchy hats. So don't feel that the whole junior and teens area is just for your daughter or your niece, even if you've reached that second-time-around age.

HOME FURNISHINGS DEPARTMENTS

Home furnishings are usually made in good-quality fabrics and attractive high-fashion colors so take a peek and you may see something that works.

A lacy table runner can make a great scarf. If you think I'm kidding, take another look. Wouldn't that work, tossed over your shoulder or loosely wrapped around your neck, or worn as a cummerbund?

Fabric napkin rings can make ponytail holders. They are elasticized and come in all patterns and colors. You can probably pick one up for about four dollars, while at the hair accessories counter something much the same would cost you from ten to twenty dollars. A large napkin can work as a neckerchief if you wash it several times to soften it, then roll it on the diagonal and tie it around your neck over a T-shirt, denim shirt, or casual blouse.

Try dried or fabric flowers. With their stems still on, you can tuck them in hatbands and through lapel buttonholes. If you remove the stems you can glue them to pin backings or fasten them to ribbon chokers.

COSMETICS DEPARTMENTS

Many years ago Estée Lauder came up with the brilliant promotional concept of a cosmetics-gift-with-purchase. Now all the cosmetics and skin care companies have these offers throughout the year.

Most of us have caught on to the idea that when we need a new lipstick and blusher, we should first check out the colors available in the line that will give us an additional gift of more cosmetics or a fashion item such as a purse. Pay attention to these offers. They are a particularly good way to acquire a large tote bag, which will see you through the summer, or an attractive cosmetics bag, which can be used as a clutch in the evening.

PARTY STORES OR STATIONERY STORES

You can use party gift wrap as a pocket square, particularly to create a seasonal mood, by choosing metallic paper in jewel tones, opalescents, gold, silver, and bronze.

The party store is also the place to find colorful ribbons, which work as hair ornaments, chokers, and necklaces.

The wax insignia that are used to seal letters can be affixed with your glue gun to plain buttons. These unusual and attractive buttons can then be sewn onto jackets or blouses as ornaments.

During the holidays it's fun to acknowledge the season but not very practical to buy something expensive that you will only wear for two or three days. Again, the party store is the place where you can find the materials to create your own holiday ornaments. I received a very favorable response to my TV segment "Trimming Your Holiday Fashions Instead of Your Tree."

Why Don't You Try These as Holiday Trims?

• Gold, silver, red, and green foil-rope tree garlands. Tack them to the hems or necklines of black or solid-color clothing.
• Pearl ropes. These tree ornaments work as necklaces, layered as thick as you like.
• Holly and ivy shoulder epaulets. Twist these wired gift-package ornaments to run along the shoulder, and tack or pin in place.
• Silver and gold stars as hair ornaments or bracelets. These thin bendable ropes of gold or silver stars are light and flexible enough to be twisted into hairdos, worn as headbands, or wrapped around the wrists of long gloves as bracelets.
• Seasonal pins. With attachable pins, which you can buy in notions stores, you can glue backing to any seasonal item and create a whole bunch of festive pins.

FABRIC STORES

You don't have to be an excellent seamstress to make use of these stores. It's easier than you think to make hatbands, pocket squares, bows, belts, and ties from pieces of fabric and use ribbons to make chokers, hair ornaments, and hat trims. There is usually a much wider choice of colors and textures to be found here than is seen when the items are already made up and on sale in department stores.

Here are some ways to use notions as accessories:

• A burlap ribbon as a trim for a straw hat, or tied around the waist of jeans or khaki or linen pants as a belt.

• Silver, gold, or rhinestone chains, or silk cording—all sold by the yard—can be tied as belts or used as necklaces.

• Buttons. These are great items to liven up simple clothes. Most of us can handle sewing on a button. By removing the plain, dull but-

tons that often come with a blouse or jacket and adding the more interesting buttons you can buy in fabric stores, you can upgrade any garment.

Mix and match buttons of varying sizes, textures, and colors for an intriguing look down the front of a blouse or jacket. Stick to the rule that they must have one of these aspects in common; then the other two can be varied. For example, try various sizes of different fabrics and textures, but all black; or different colors, various sizes, but all bone or all fabric.

Use buttons to express mood—wood is sporty and rustic; pewter is sharp and continental; velvet is romantic.

• Gold braiding and gold fabric stars. Sew these on plain jackets to create your own military look.

MUSEUM STORES

Museum stores have really grown in popularity in recent years. They are not only attached to museums; free-standing stores associated with various institutions can be discovered in malls around the country. They display a wide variety of interesting merchandise, much of it inspired by the themes of their exhibits.

They have collections of contemporary and period jewelry, which you may want to own or give as gifts. They stock not just T-shirts but under-, outer-, and even bedroom wear. Their tote bags come in attractive designs as do their scarves and handkerchiefs.

MILITARY AND WAR-SURPLUS STORES

Military uniforms have an enduring influence on fashion.

Ralph Lauren is always finding new ways to work soldier and sailor influences into his clothes. One of his most successful looks combines the British army tradition with Far Eastern sarongs, and he's always loved epaulet and braid trim on classic navy blazers.

Donna Karan has also often used the military look without losing her feminine touch. She has designed navy pea coats and jackets with

epaulets, and added brass buttons and officer stripes to many of her garments.

Most people can't afford to go all the way with these designers' looks, especially at their prices, but if you hunt in the military and war-surplus stores you can find uniforms and the accessories to go with them.

This is a good place to look for berets, too.

Knapsacks can be used as purses—a very up-to-date fashion statement. Lauren Hutton has used this look cleverly.

Dog tags work as jewelry items, as do old medals and pins.

Military canvas belts work well, cinched low over long tunics and blouses.

SPORTING GOODS STORES

These are the stores where the real enthusiasts shop for their fishing tackle and hunting and camping supplies.

In the fishing department, the canvas fishing bags make wonderful shoulder pouches. Wicker fishing baskets in small sizes make unusual summer purses.

In the hunting department, cartridge bags, in green canvas with suede or brown leather straps and trim, complement your weekend sportswear. Olive canvas satchels, with net-mesh outer pockets and adjustable straps, are ideal shoulder bags and backpacks.

ATHLETIC STORES

These are the places to look for baseball and cycling hats, bandana scarves and headbands, fanny packs, and wide leather work-out belts to wear over knits and bodysuits—they look better if you distress them rather than wearing them brand-new, so that you look like a serious exerciser with style, rather than just someone trying to get in on the act.

Another idea is to wear a mile calculator or pulse or heart-rate monitor on a long cord as a medallion.

HARDWARE STORES

Avant-garde designer Jean Paul Gaultier draped links of hardware-store chain around the chignons of his models. I've used the toilet pull chain, which you buy by the yard in either silver or brass, to hang my favorite charms on. This looks best when worn extra long.

The hardware store is the place to find the buttercup-color chamois you use for washing your car. You can cut it into strips to use as a headband or ponytail holder, or cut off a piece to use as a pocket square. Chamois looks wonderful worn with all the sun-bleached, faded pastels for spring or summer or with an oatmeal-color business suit. You can also leave it whole, roll it, and use it as a Western-style scarf with your denims.

FIVE-AND-TENS

The five-and-ten is a more affordable alternative to the department store for casual accessories you need just to see you through the current season. At these stores you can find white cotton socks, flip-flop beach sandals, clear plastic beach totes, cowboy bandanas for a dollar, and good tortoiseshell hair accessories.

FLEA MARKETS, THRIFT SHOPS, ANTIQUE STORES, SWAP MEETS, AND ESTATE AND GARAGE SALES

Going to these alternative shopping sites is an amusing way to spend a day. The family will usually enjoy it too, because there is such a variety of items on display that everyone can find something of interest to remind them of past fads, encourage new ideas for collecting, and entice them to buy gifts for friends. While your son is considering toy trains as an alternative to his latest video game, or your husband is reading the old comic books he loved as a kid, you can hunt for all the accessories you want.

Old watches, wide 1940s ties, Bakelite sunglasses, mother-of-pearl jewelry, beaded purses, old political campaign or sports buttons are all in plentiful supply at most of these places.

The stalls that carry old linen and home furnishings are always a good place to browse. Bits of old lace or handmade cotton doilies and antimacassars make good pocket squares or can be used to trim a hat.

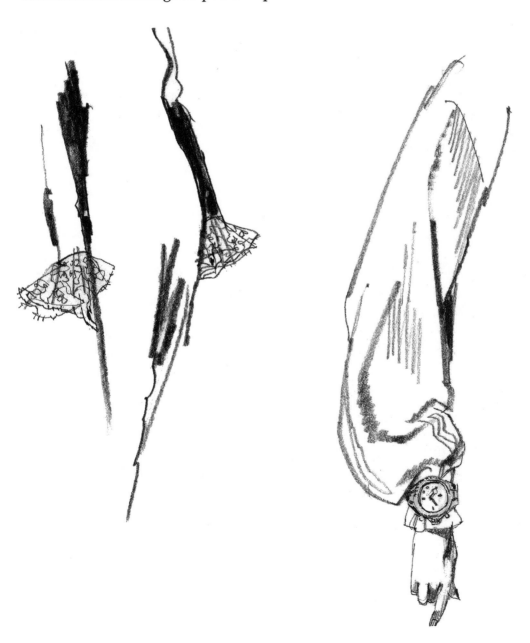

Old pieces of silver flatware can be bent into pins or adapted to earrings. If you are handy with soldering or glue you can do this yourself, but a local jeweler will be happy to help you otherwise.

Look for old leather handbags and luggage, eyeglass frames, watch fobs to wear as necklaces—a very high-fashion trend—and pocket watches. These watches can be pinned on a piece of ribbon as civic and military decorations often are and then worn as brooches, or they can be attached to watch chains and worn looped to your belt and threaded into your pocket.

If you find a wonderful old hat that is bent and crinkled, you can re-structure it with steaming. Find a bowl that approximates your head size, place the hat over it, and put it in your bathroom to steam when the shower or bathtub is running.

Gloves are another item you will find in plentiful supply at these alternative shopping sites, particularly evening gloves, which were once de rigueur at formal events.

All these items can be found in good condition if you look carefully.

You can re-create any favorite look from the past, and have fun imagining the history of the item you've chosen, but you can also find new versions of most of these ideas, because modern artists and vendors often take stalls at swap meets to sell their wares.

Perhaps there is a vendor who will paint a white baseball hat with a favorite image—a picture of the horse you ride, or scenes of the beach or the mountains where you'll wear this cap. Perhaps there are new tie-dyed scarves in better condition than the old ones also on sale.

Wherever you are shopping, use your imagination and you'll find it much easier and more affordable than you thought to pick up on trends and make them your own. This way you'll be a trend setter, not simply a trend follower. Diane Keaton is among the most interesting dressers in Hollywood, and she is an avid shopper at flea markets and swap meets.

Love That Accessory Style!

Remember the all-important rule that should be applied to any accessory you buy: If you feel hesitant or unsure, don't buy it.

You must really love it in order for it to be perfect for you.

If you truly love an accessory, whether it is the latest, trendiest fad or an antique relic, you will wear it with confidence. Confidence is the essence of style. When you are confident, your individuality will shine through, reflecting your own unique style.

In their search for style, women too often forget about their individuality, believing that style is acquired by chasing after fads and fancies, rather than listening to their own inner voices and building on their sense of self.

Always remember that the solution to achieving style is right in your own backyard, or more precisely, in your own drawers and closets—the places where you keep your accessories. More than your basic clothes, these accessories work to create the true expression of your individual style.

Because you've chosen the accessories you love, each time you put them on you will find pleasure in the way they look and in the way they enhance your overall appearance—that wide, worn brown-leather belt with the distressed brass buckle; that oversized man's black sports watch; that antique locket hung on a satin ribbon. People will admire your accessories, ask where you found them, and comment on how well you wear them. They'll also love the way you mix and match your accessories—those gold, silver, and Lucite bangles, one a precious family heirloom, one purchased at a street stall, one a memento from your recent vacation, all hung on a single wrist; those ropes of pearls, worn with a Museum of Modern Art charm on a long chain bought at the hardware store; that antique purse, the leather enhanced by years of polishing, large enough to work as a briefcase with your contemporary business suit; that circular rhinestone pin at the neck of your blue denim shirt; that flowing, drifting lace scarf softening the lines of your tailored navy pin-stripe coatdress.

The confidence you have acquired from knowing that your accessory wardrobe contains both the essentials and the unique will enable you to create stylish combinations easily and quickly each time you dress. You'll love the style they give you. It's easy, it's your own personal style, it's "Quickstyle."

ADDENDUM

CHECK OUT YOUR ACCESSORY STYLE!

There are four ways to determine if you have learned the secrets of achieving style that I have talked about in this book.

First, open up your closets and chest of drawers. Can you identify and access your accessories easily?

Second, look over your new clothing purchases. Are you buying clothes that are solid-color classics without a lot of fancy trim, details, or decoration? Have you been wearing these new clothes often while the busy, print outfits you used to favor gather dust?

Third, check out your accessories. Do you now have the essential accessories I recommend—jewelry, belts, purses, gloves, nylons, and shoes—that go with the clothes in your wardrobe as the foundation of your style?

Fourth and finally, take an extra look at yourself in the mirror once you are dressed. Do you look more striking than you used to because there are touches of the unexpected in your choice of accessories—perhaps four varied silver pins clustered on one lapel, instead of only one; perhaps a lace scarf, folded and tucked into the neck of your dress, rather than a conventional print draped over your shoulder?

If you can answer yes to all these questions then you have discovered that getting dressed every day, for any occasion, is an enjoyable adventure rather than a chore. You will feel good about the way you have combined your accessories with your clothes. You will feel confident about the way you look. You will get compliments from your friends, co-workers, and family. You will find that other women now ask you where you found that wonderful pin or how you attached that gold chain to your leather belt, or whether your watch is a real antique. You will be aware that your money seems to be going farther because you've invested both in classics, which have lasting value, and unique items, which you love so much and which work in so many attractive ways that you will never want to stop wearing them.

This confidence and the understanding of how to achieve your own style easily will make you look good and feel good about yourself. Congratulations for being adventurous and achieving the realization of your own unique style.

Don't let the adventure end. Keep on investing in your style by being constantly on the lookout for wonderful items to add to your wardrobe. Stay in style by using accessories, rather than trendy outfits. Style with accessories—that's "Quickstyle."

ABOUT THE AUTHOR

CHRISTINE KUNZELMAN *created the Panache Appearance Studios in Los Angeles in 1979, specializing in all aspects of appearance for men and women. She went on to become fashion and beauty editor of KABC Talk Radio and KABC-TV Eyewitness News in Los Angeles, and became a familiar face in California as a fashion reporter on* AM Los Angeles *and* AM San Francisco. *She has since become a national television personality with her regular appearances on* Live With Regis and Kathie Lee *and other daytime talk shows, as well as her work as contributing correspondent to the* Today *show. Kunzelman is also a spokesperson for many of the country's leading fashion and beauty companies. In her private image consultation business, she advises politicians and TV and movie personalities.*